East Anglia

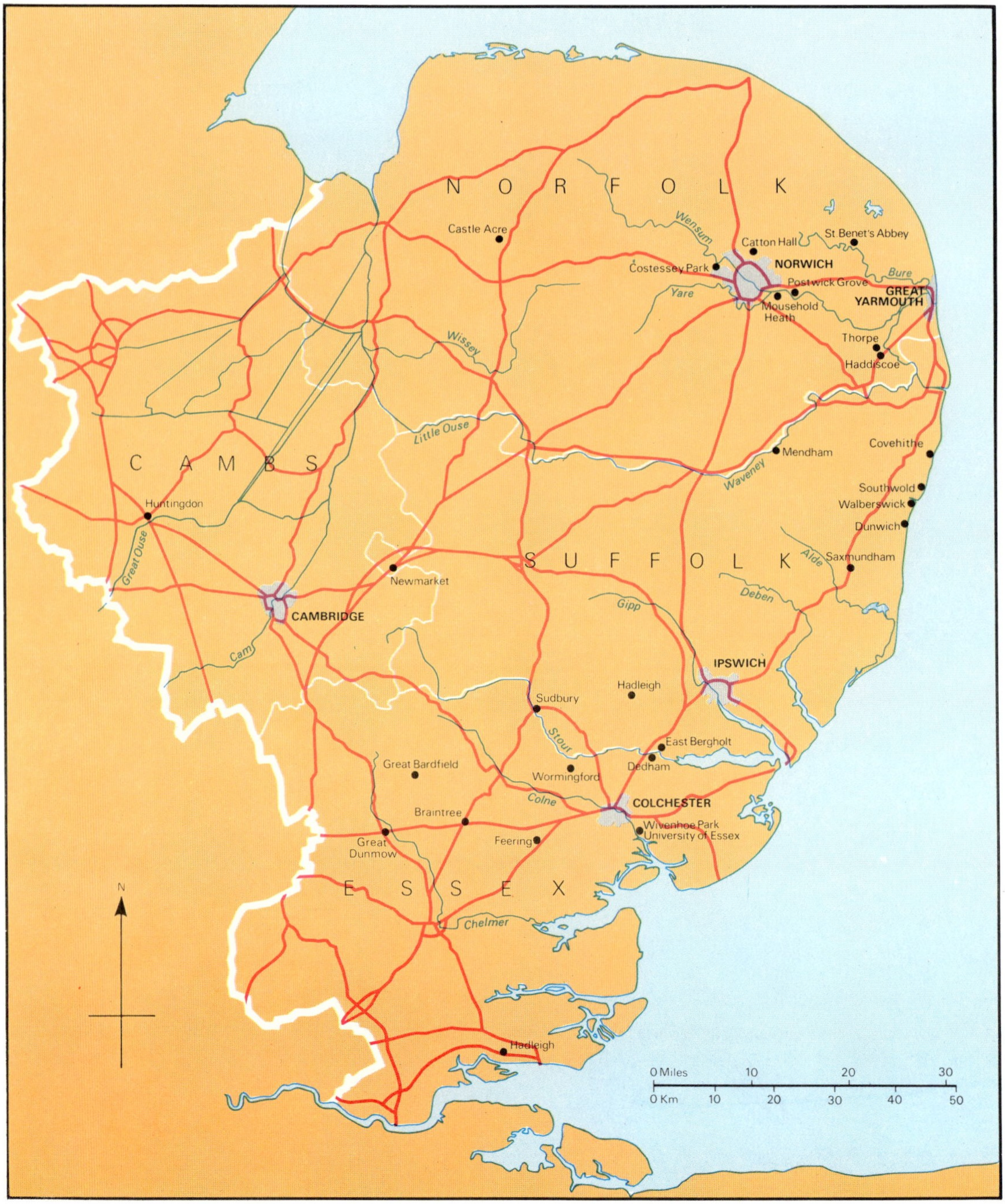
NORFOLK
Castle Acre
Catton Hall
St Benet's Abbey
Wensum
Costessey Park
NORWICH
Bure
Postwick Grove
GREAT YARMOUTH
Yare
Mousehold Heath
Wissey
Thorpe
Haddiscoe
Little Ouse
CAMBS
Covehithe
Mendham
Waveney
Southwold
Walberswick
Huntingdon
Dunwich
Great Ouse
SUFFOLK
Alde
Saxmundham
Newmarket
Deben
Gipp
CAMBRIDGE
Cam
IPSWICH
Hadleigh
Sudbury
Stour
East Bergholt
Dedham
Great Bardfield
Wormingford
Colne
COLCHESTER
Braintree
Wivenhoe Park
University of Essex
Great Dunmow
Feering
N
ESSEX
Chelmer
Hadleigh
0 Miles
10
20
30
0 Km
10
20
30
40
50

INTRODUCTION

East Anglian art is characterized by a predominance of landscape painting and associated with two centres of activity: the Stour Valley and Norwich. The stretch of the Stour Valley between Flatford and Nayland was called 'Constable's Country' even in the artist's own day, and can hardly be visited without one's being conscious of his paintings. But Constable was not the only artist, nor even the first, to paint here. His most illustrious predecessor was Thomas Gainsborough, who, though principally a portraitist, always regarded landscape painting as his true vocation, and did many views around his native Sudbury;

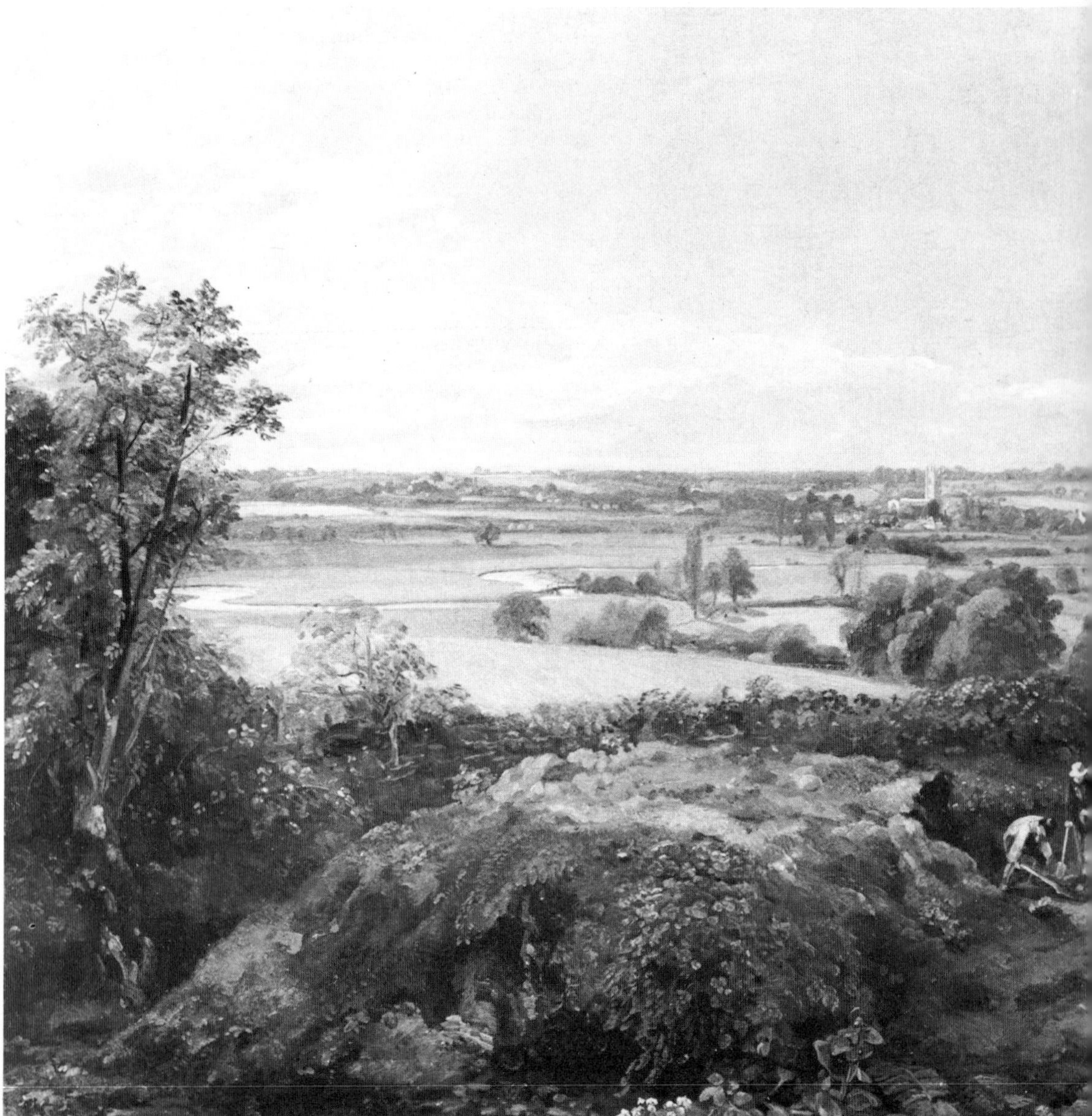

when Constable explored East Anglia he was aware of Gainsborough 'in every hedge and hollow tree'. The Stour Valley also attracted the two most important East Anglian artists of this century, Sir Alfred Munnings and John Nash. Munnings, immensely successful and one of the greatest horse-painters this century, spent most of his life in the grand Castle House at Dedham. Nash, in contrast, lived in a modest and primitive cottage just outside the village of Wormingford. It is unlikely that the term 'Nash's Country' will ever be coined, but the area around Wormingford calls his paintings to mind in a remarkable way and still remains almost as secluded and unspoilt as when he painted it.

Norwich has a very different countryside, which in its unmitigated flatness can be closely compared with Holland. Accordingly, many of its painters have felt a strong affinity with the great Dutch masters, and this was brought out by the patron Dawson Turner when discussing John Crome's *Moonrise on the Yare*: 'born and educated in a country peculiarly distinguished by the flatness of its surface, and there having always lived, and there consequently formed his style, it is not wonderful that his [Crome's] productions should approach in their character to those of the School of our opposite neighbours upon the Continent.' The Norwich School was the most cohesive and insular of all the regional schools of painting in England. Owing to Norwich's rather isolated position, many of its artists, including Crome, only worked, and were known, locally. John Sell Cotman, the other leading painter of the school, was constantly frustrated in his attempts to gain national recognition, and his ambitiousness caused him considerable unhappiness. Norfolk remained singularly unadventurous in its patronage. The buyers on whom the Norwich School depended were simply local men who wanted representations of the countryside and places they knew and loved.

East Anglia's strong tradition of landscape painting in the eighteenth and nineteenth centuries has been maintained into modern times. In the 1880s Wilson Steer, while staying at Walberswick, applied a highly original, Impressionist vision to the Suffolk coast. Steer's imaginative experimentation at this period was exceptional in his own career and has found no sequel in the history of East Anglian painting. Later artists have been responsible for the continuity in the practice of landscape painting this century, but they have not been in the forefront of contemporary art. Many of them, such as Sir John Arnesby Brown, Sir Cedric Morris, John Aldridge, or Peter Coker, are little known outside the area and, like their celebrated East Anglian forbears, have attracted a principally local patronage.

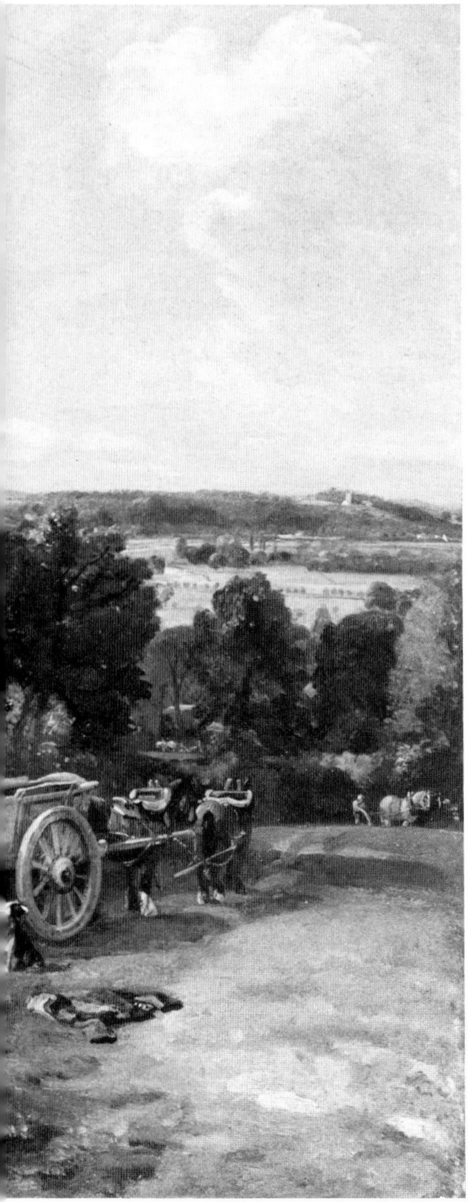

John Constable
The Stour Valley and Dedham Church
1814–15; oil on canvas, 55·2 × 78·1 cm
Museum of Fine Arts, Boston

Castle Acre, *Norfolk*

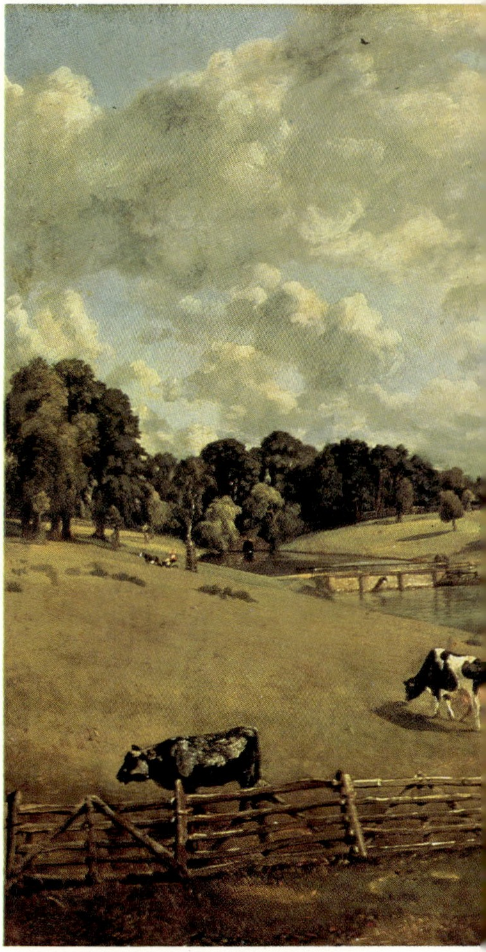

Castle Acre Priory was visited by John Sell Cotman in August 1804, just after his first stay with Dawson Turner at Covehithe and Yarmouth (q.v.). The letter that Cotman wrote to Turner from Castle Acre reveals his excitable nature: 'Cove Hithe – pish, my dear Sir, must not be named with this. Oh! it is tremendously fine. Come! Come! Come! ye admirers of Beauties and escape from those galling chains of fashioned follies – Yarmouth Ball, a bad partner at cards or – a Blaydon Bog. Come! Come!' Cotman included a rough sketch of the west front of the priory, which he hoped would give Turner 'some little idea of its beauty'. The following week was spent assiduously sketching the site. Nine days after leaving the area, however, Cotman could write ecstatic praise about Croyland Abbey in Lincolnshire and find that 'Castle Acre to it is as nothing'.

Colchester, *Essex*

In the late summer of 1816 John Constable stayed at Wivenhoe Park (now occupied by the University of Essex) as the guest of General Francis Slater-Rebow, who commissioned from him a view of the house from across the lake (National Gallery, Washington). This area of the park is rather more thickly wooded now, but the site of the picture can still be located without difficulty. At the same time as *Wivenhoe*

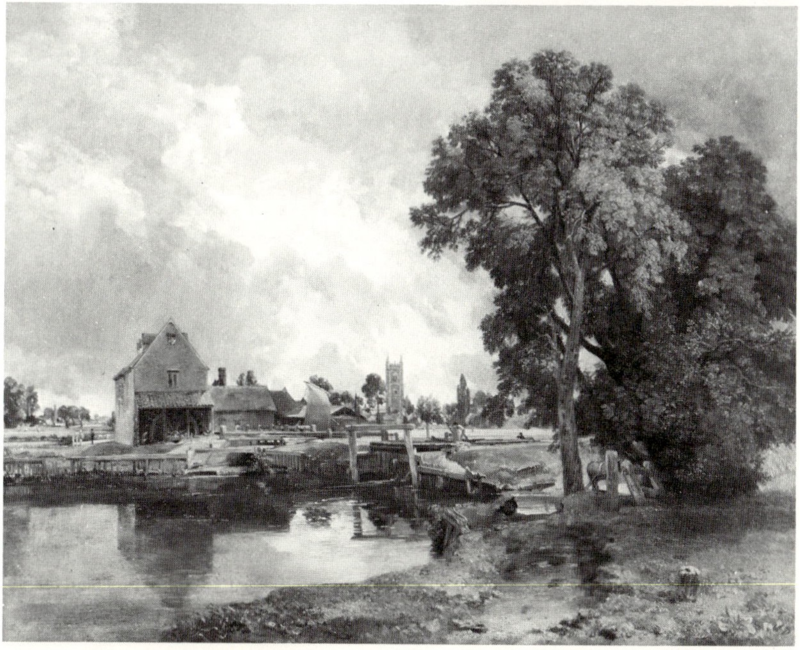

John Constable
Dedham Lock and Mill
1819; oil on canvas, 71·1 × 90·2 cm
Private collection

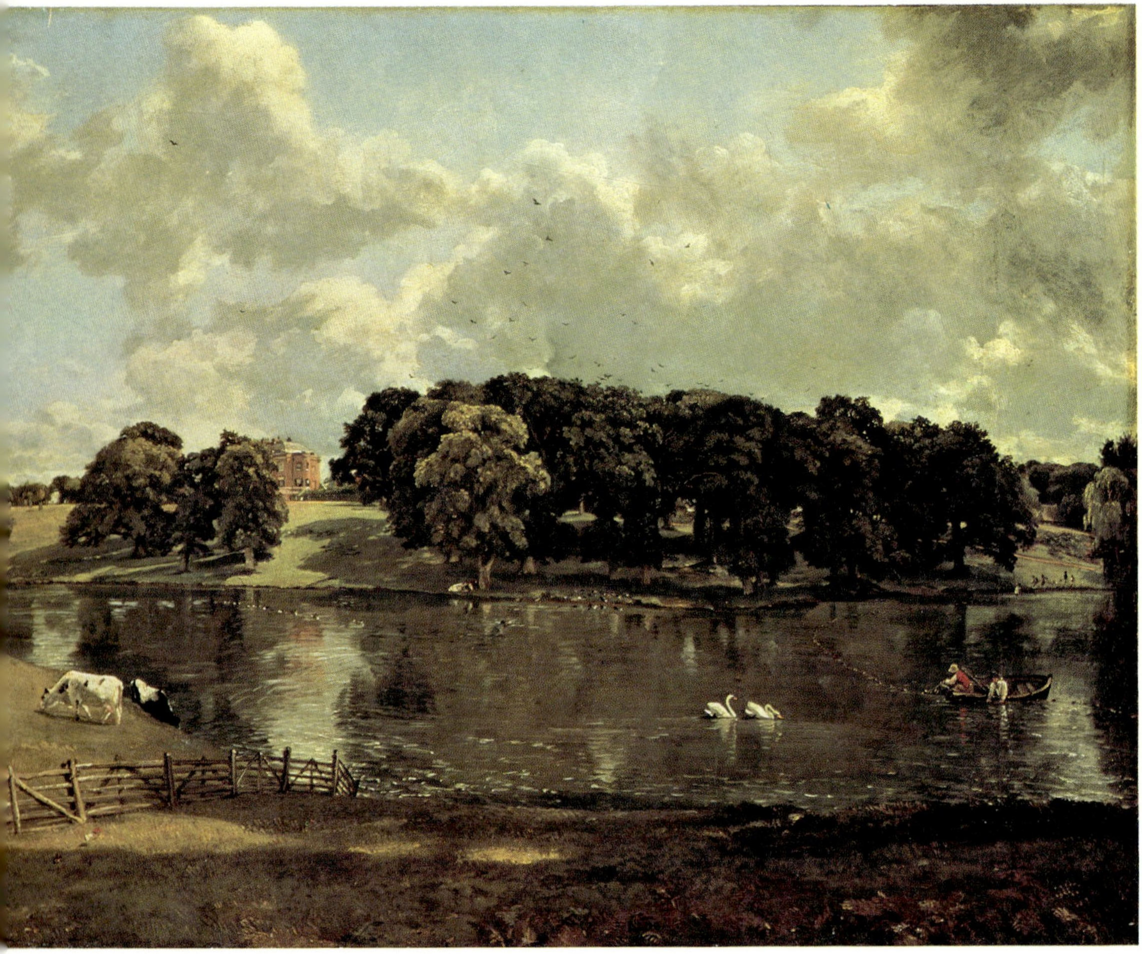

Park Constable painted a scene at Alresford, the General's other estate near Colchester, featuring 'The Quarters', an exotic eighteenth-century fishing-lodge. This and its bosky surroundings also remain much as they were in Constable's time.

Dedham, *Suffolk*

John Constable's father owned the mill at Dedham (now replaced by modern mill-buildings) and Constable made several paintings of it. Dedham Church was another of his favourite motifs, featuring both in paintings of the mill and in more general Stour Valley landscapes such as the Boston *View of Dedham*, which is taken from a point near East Bergholt (q.v.). The artist was a devout Christian and seems to have regarded Dedham Church as a symbol of God's beneficent presence in the agricultural landscape.

Another artist associated with Dedham is Sir Alfred Munnings. Munnings was brought up in Mendham (q.v.) but his father came from Stoke-by-Nayland in the Stour Valley. An early visit to the area in company with his father made a powerful impression on the young artist: 'We found it beautiful, unspoilt as in the days of Constable.' But it was many years later, in 1920, that Munnings finally settled in Dedham, at Castle House. Described by the artist as 'the house of my dreams', it is now open to the public for part of the year and contains over a hundred of his paintings and sketches. Munnings's excitement at purchasing Castle House is vividly related in Volume II of his autobiography, *The Second Burst* (1951): 'I was riveted by the drawing-room, with its Regency bow windows looking out across peaceful paddocks with chestnut trees and cows grazing.' He also rented land near the house, giving ample space for his beloved horses, which were the principal source of inspiration for his art. Munnings's immense popularity as a pain-

John Constable
Wivenhoe Park, Essex
1816–17; oil on canvas, 56·1 × 101·2 cm
National Gallery of Art, Washington (Widener Collection)

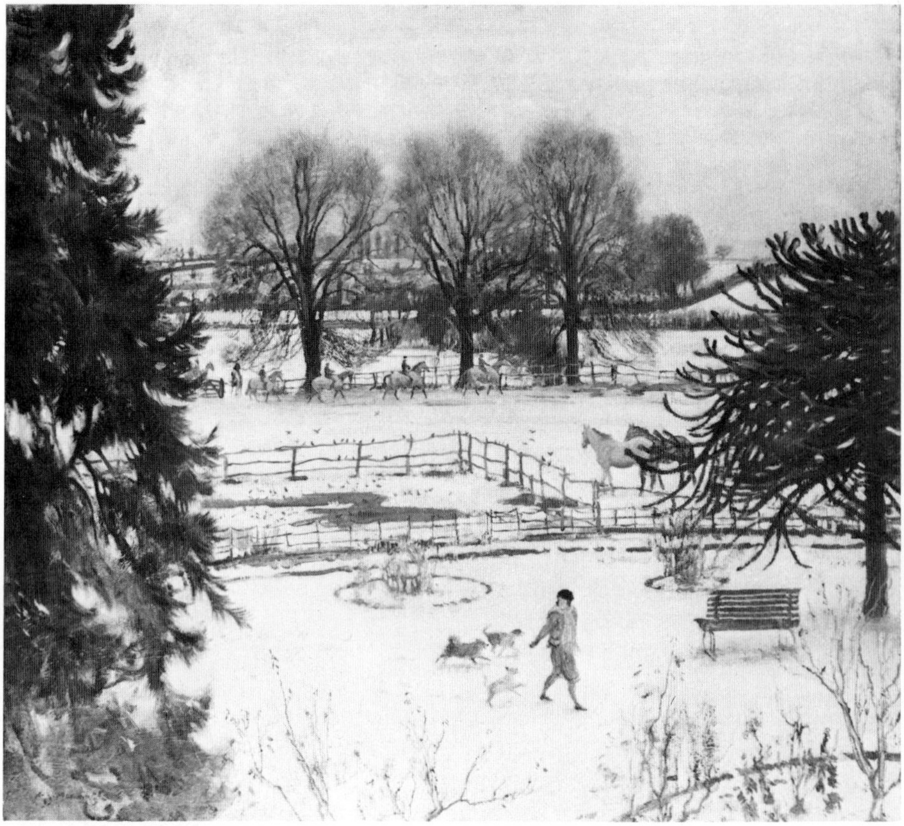

Alfred Munnings
From my Bedroom Window
1930; oil on canvas, 91·5 × 101·5 cm
Tate Gallery, London

ter dates from the time of his move to Dedham. In 1944 he was knighted and elected President of the Royal Academy.

East Bergholt, *Suffolk*

No part of the English landscape is more strongly associated with the name of one artist than is the Stour Valley with that of John Constable. He was the second son of Golding Constable of East Bergholt House. Golding came from a long line of Suffolk and Essex yeomen and was the proprietor of two watermills on the Stour, at Flatford and Dedham (q.v.); in addition to running the mills, he managed the transportation of flour down-river to his own wharf on the estuary at Mistley, and thence to London. As a youth, John worked in the family business and acquired a familiarity with the workings of mills and locks which informs his paintings of scenes along the river. He spent much of his spare time sketching and painting, often in company with John Dunthorne, a local amateur artist. He also received some early encouragement from the prominent patron and connoisseur Sir George Beaumont, whose mother lived at Dedham.

At the age of twenty-two Constable obtained his father's consent to take up art as a fulltime occupation and was soon afterwards admitted to the Royal Academy Schools in London. As a student he came to be critical of contemporary landscape painting, considering it artificial and too dependent on the Old Masters: 'there is room enough', he wrote to Dunthorne in 1802, 'for a natural painture'. Constable therefore took a small property at East Bergholt for use as a studio and began to spend long periods there each summer, making studies from nature in his native countryside. He continued, however, to live for the larger part of the year in London, and regularly submitted pictures to the annual Academy exhibitions. These were fairly modest works – watercolours and small oils – until the appearance of his first large-scale exhibition picture, *Dedham Vale, Morning* (private collection), in 1811. After this he produced Stour Valley landscapes of increasing size and grandeur, culminating in a series of six-foot canvases exhibited between 1819 and 1825.

Constable's mother died in 1815 and his father in the following year. His inheritance enabled him finally to marry Maria Bick-

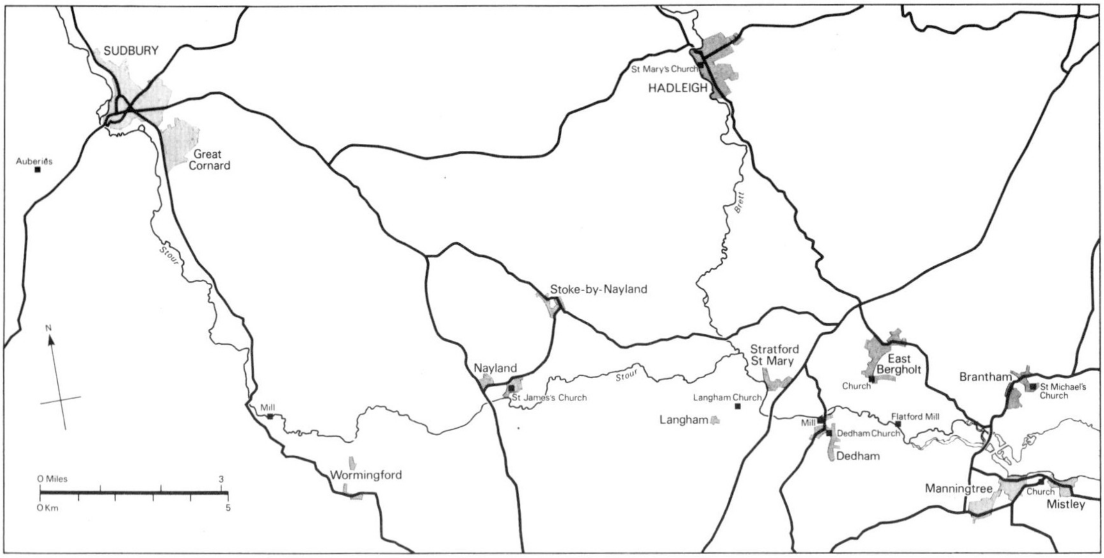

The Stour Valley

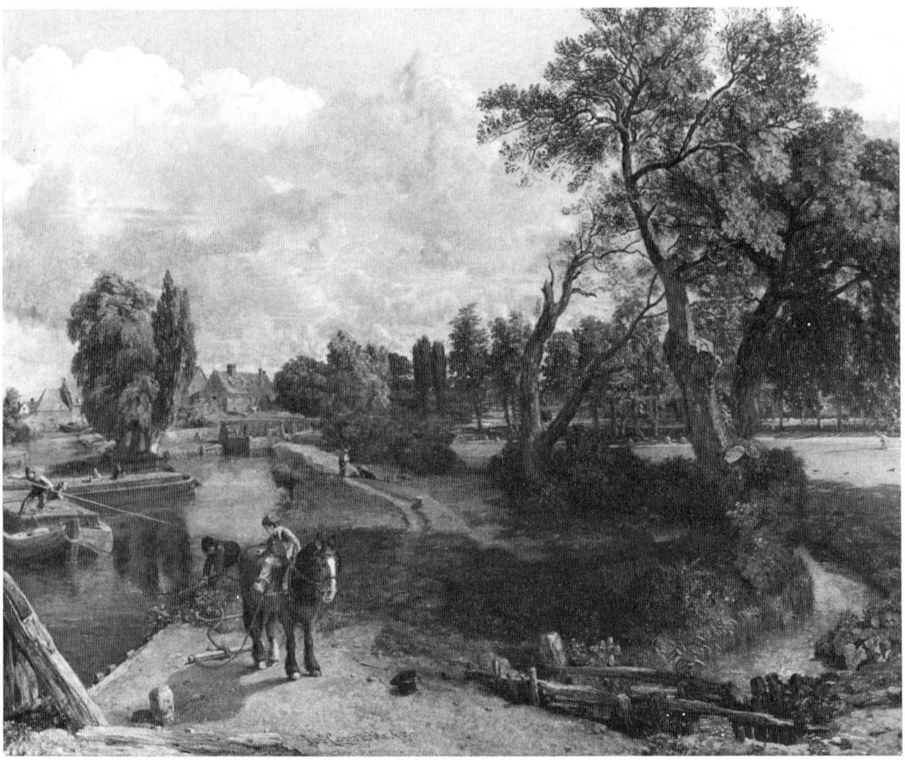

John Constable
Flatford Mill
1817; oil on canvas,
101·6 × 127·1 cm
Tate Gallery,
London

nell, the couple's seven-year-long courtship having been hampered by opposition from Maria's grandfather, who was the rector of East Bergholt. Henceforth Constable spent less and less time in Suffolk – the summer of 1817 saw his last long visit – and his Stour Valley scenes of the 1820s and '30s were largely based on earlier sketches and memories. These works of his middle and old age are suffused with a nostalgia for childhood experiences that suggests comparison with his contemporary, Wordsworth. He wrote in 1821: 'I associate my "careless boyhood" to all that lies on the banks of the Stour.'

East Bergholt House, in which the artist

was born, stood on the east side of Church Street. To it were attached some thirty-seven acres of pasture and arable land, parts of which are lovingly portrayed in the paintings of 1815 known as *Golding Constable's Flower Garden* and *Golding Constable's Kitchen Garden*. The house itself was demolished in the mid nineteenth century and now only a utility wing, converted into cottages, remains.

As the large crowds of tourists that visit the place suggest, the best-known site in 'Constable's Country' is Flatford Mill. The artist seems first to have concentrated his attention on this area around 1810–12, when he made a series of sketches in oil on paper. The later and larger composition called simply *Flatford Mill* shows the lock just above the mill from a position up-river on the Essex bank. The viewpoint is slightly elevated, being taken from the slope up to a footbridge (the present bridge is a later

John Constable
Golding Constable's Kitchen Garden
1815; oil on canvas,
33 × 50·8 cm
Ipswich Museum

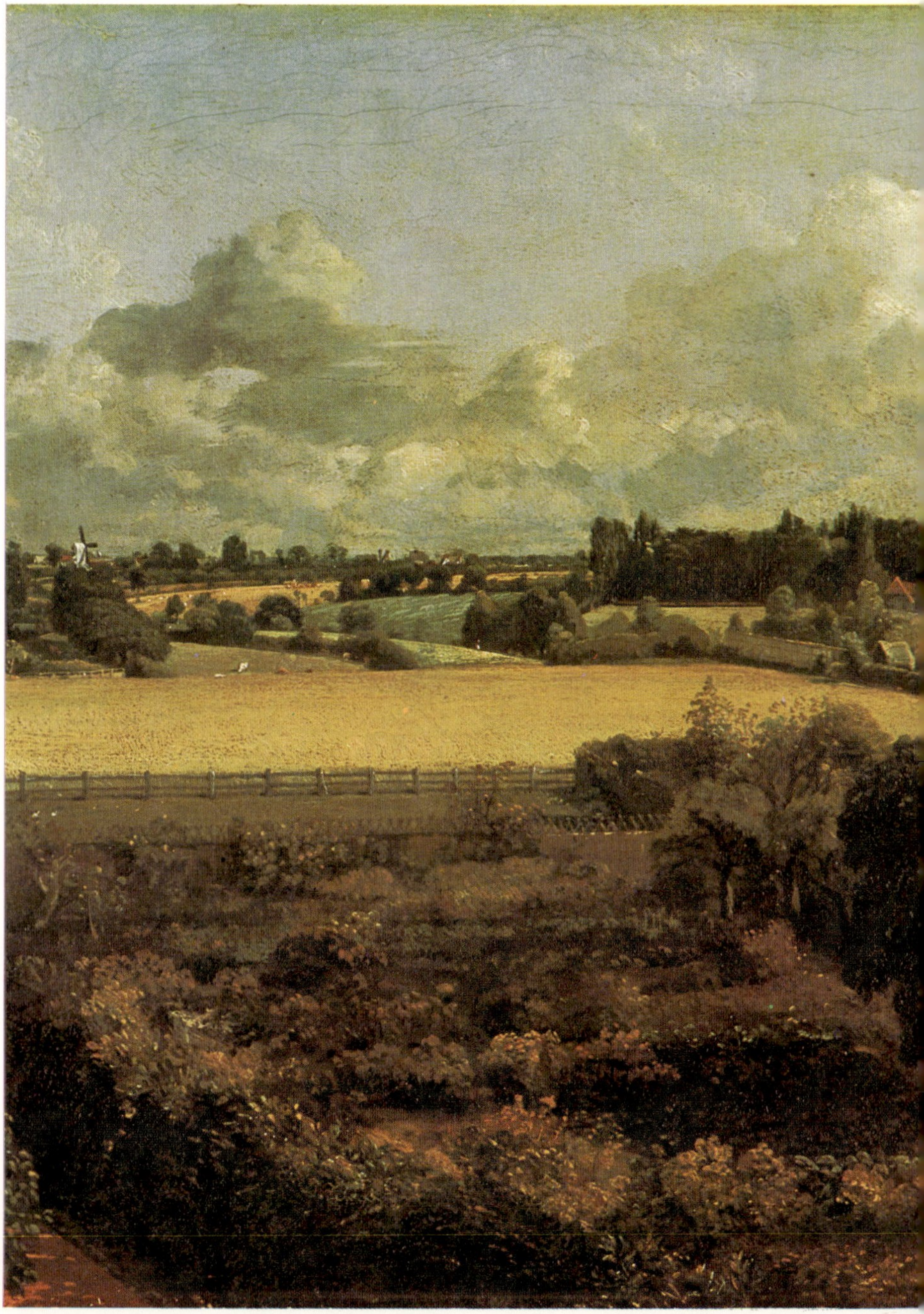

replacement). On the left of the picture, barges are being disconnected from the towing-horse so that they can be poled under the bridge. The mill-buildings are visible in the distance, beyond the lock.

The most famous of Constable's 'six-footers', *The Haywain*, is a view down-river from the mill, including the house of Willy Lott, a local farmer. The house was restored in the early part of this century and presented to the nation; it is now leased by the National Trust to the Field Studies Council for use as a Field Centre, where courses on painting, local ecology and history are held. Willy Lott's house was one of Constable's favourite motifs: he made numerous oil sketches of it during the second decade of the century, one or more of which may have been used in preparing the composition of *The Haywain*. The picture shows an empty wain fording the millstream on its way to collect another load

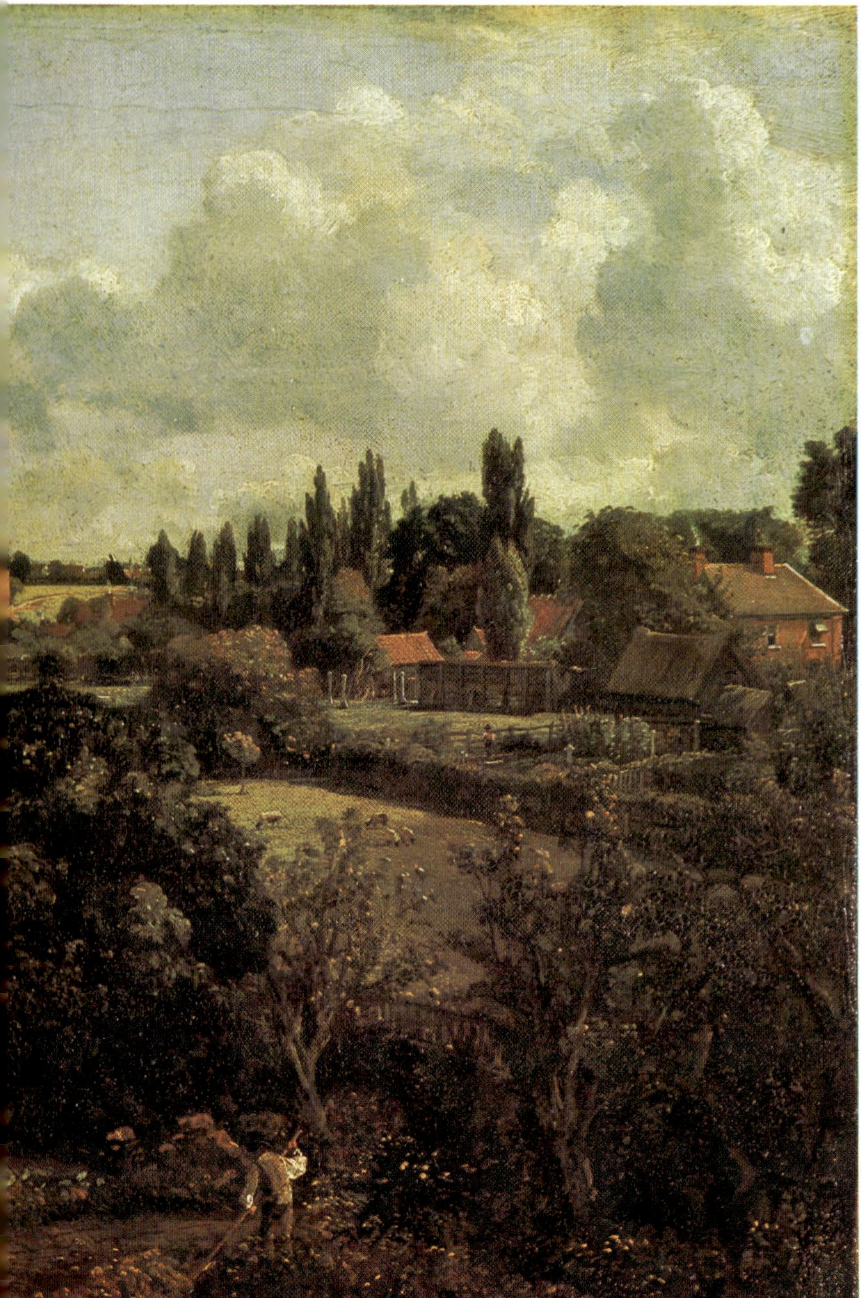

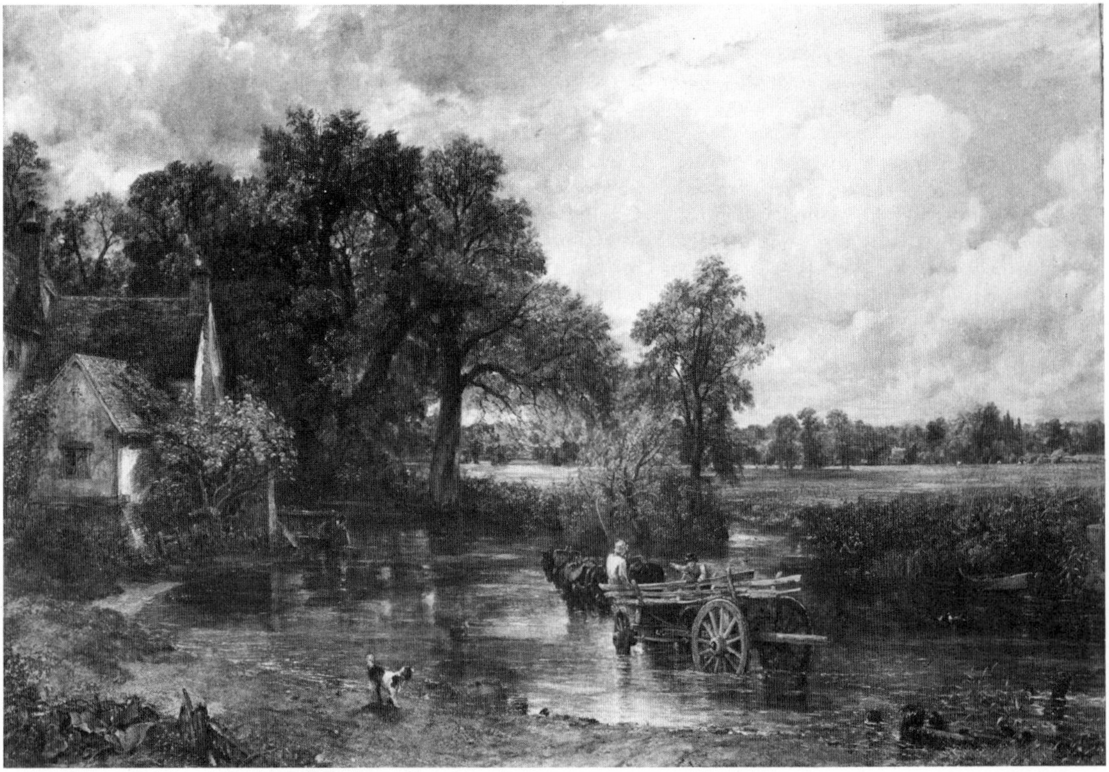

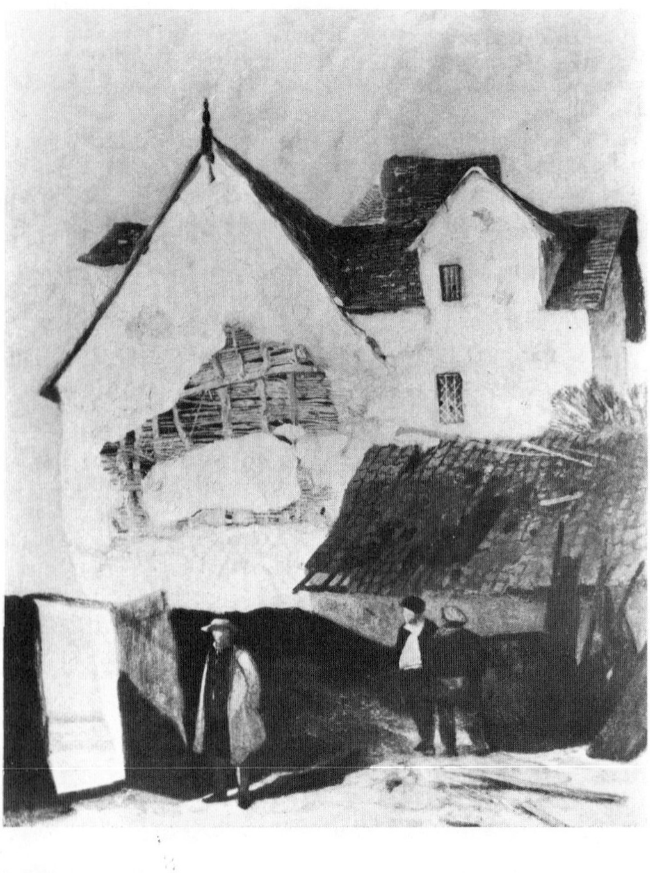

from the distant fields, in which labourers can be seen at work. In order that these should be visible, Constable omitted a row of trees on the far side of the stream. *The Haywain* and *Flatford Mill* demonstrate Constable's concern with representing the 'working landscape'. He delighted in both natural and man-made features of the river scene: 'the sound of water escaping from Mill dams, etc., Willows, Old rotten Banks, slimy posts, & brickwork – I love such things . . .'

An uncharacteristic work of Constable's, an altarpiece depicting *Christ Blessing the Children*, is in St Michael's Church, Brantham. It was probably commissioned through Dr Rhudde, who was rector of Brantham as well as East Bergholt, and was well disposed towards Constable until the artist became romantically involved with his granddaughter. Constable also painted altarpieces for St James's, Nayland (still *in situ*) and St Michael's, Manningtree (now removed to All Saints, Feering, Essex).

Great Bardfield, *Essex*

The illustrator and muralist Edward Bawden has had a lifelong association with Essex. He was born in Braintree in 1903 and moved in 1932 to Great Bardfield, near by.

At that date he and his friend, the illustrator Eric Ravilious, began renting a Georgian red-brick house, situated on the main street of the village and called simply Brick House. This Bawden used at first as a weekend retreat, but in 1935 he became a permanent resident, staying until his wife's death in 1970, when he moved to Saffron Walden. A great friend of his is John Aldridge, a fellow Royal Academician who still lives in the village, in Place House; the two artists share a passionate interest in gardening.

In the 1950s Great Bardfield blossomed into a well-known art centre, and many professional painters, potters and weavers took up residence in the village. During this period there was a series of much publicized collective summer exhibitions, when the artists opened up their gardens and studios to the public. One artist who settled in the vicinity at this time was the versatile Michael Ayrton, who worked not only as a painter, sculptor and etcher, but also as an art critic, novelist, broadcaster, theatrical designer and film director; he lived at Bradfields in Toppesfield until his death in 1975.

Great Yarmouth, *Norfolk*

The years of England's war with France (1793–1815), which disastrously affected Yarmouth's importance as a port, were, as in the case of Norwich, the greatest ones in its history as an artistic centre. This was largely due to the influence of one man, Dawson Turner, one of the most significant East Anglian patrons. Turner was a wealthy banker, whose father James had founded Gurney and Turner's Bank in Great Yarmouth; the site of Bank House, where the family lived and worked, is now marked by the mid-nineteenth-century Barclays Bank, situated on the quay just across the bridge from Southtown. Turner's interest in art was obsessive, and he approached the subject with a rigorous, businesslike spirit. The painter B. R. Haydon described his life as 'one incessant scene of fact-collecting.... He was an immense living index.'

Turner's wife, in common with many of the cultured women of her time, had artistic aspirations, and to encourage these he employed the Norwich artist John Crome as a drawing-master; later Crome extended his teaching to their two elder daughters. But it was with Crome's rival, John Sell Cotman, that Turner was most closely associated. Exactly when and how he came into contact with Cotman is not known, but in the summer of 1804 Cotman was already on very friendly terms with him, staying for a short period at his country house at Covehithe and later at Bank House. Cotman had a speciality in architectural and

OPPOSITE ABOVE:
John Constable
The Haywain
1821; oil on canvas, 130·2 × 185·4 cm
National Gallery, London

OPPOSITE, BELOW:
John Sell Cotman
Old Houses at Gorleston
Oil on canvas, 45·7 × 35·6 cm
Castle Museum, Norwich

John Crome
Moonrise on the Yare
c. 1811–16; oil on canvas, 71·1 × 111·1 cm
Tate Gallery, London

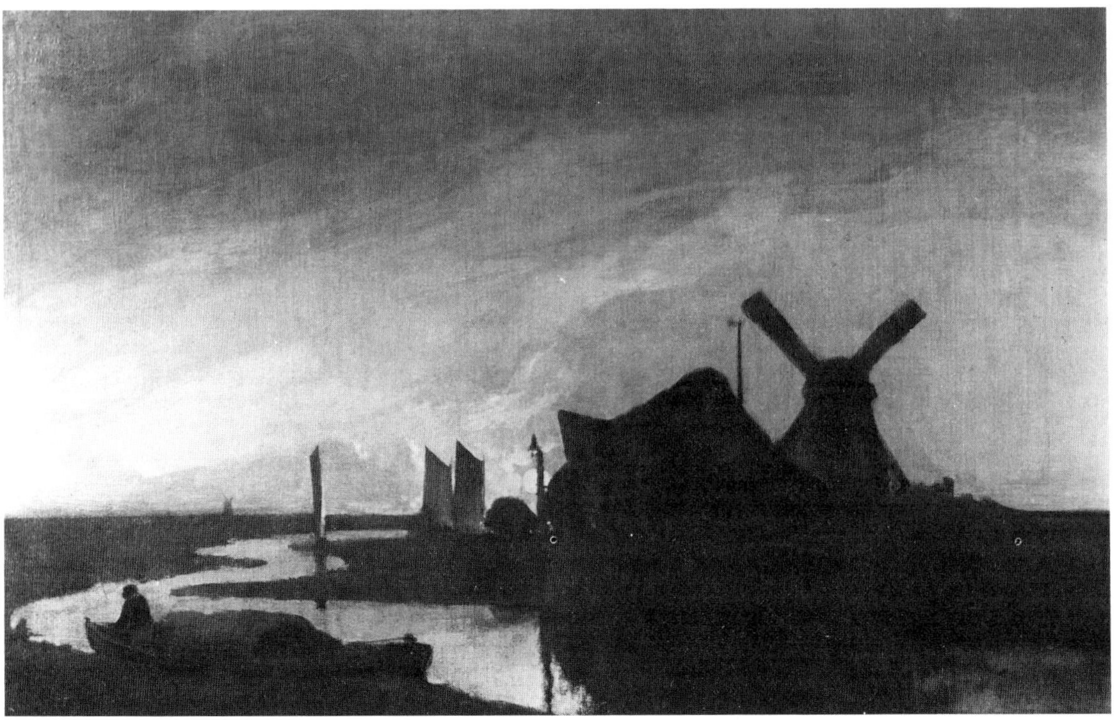

archaeological drawings, which particularly appealed to Turner, and it was probably this factor that led to his eventually taking over Crome's position as drawing-master.

By the end of 1811 Turner was encouraging Cotman to leave Norwich, where he had still to establish himself successfully, and come to Yarmouth. The correspondence between the two at this time throws considerable light on Cotman's difficult character. He was an inveterate snob, and reluctant to move to what he considered more provincial surroundings, especially as he felt that the series of etchings on which he was engaged – representations of the major architectural sites of Norfolk – would bring him sudden fame. Another factor was his habitual fussiness as to the house where he lived: 'Then I should be sorry to remove to a house smaller than the one I am in now. And to get one over the Bridge, which I should prefer, the rent would be double if not treble my present rent.' Turner, with characteristic common sense, forced Cotman to see the matter in a more realistic light, and the artist capitulated, provided that he could 'meet with a pleasant and respectable house – not too small – in some quiet situation'. The house that Turner found for him still survives as No. 83 Southtown Road (marked by a plaque): not, needless to say, on the right side of the river, but a necessary solution, considering the artist's financial situation.

The years Cotman and his family spent at Yarmouth were relatively stable ones. Much of his work as an archaeological draughtsman dates from this period, including many views of Normandy, which he visited, with members of Dawson Turner's family, on three occasions, in 1817, 1818 and 1820. Cotman was, however, too ambitious, and in spite of repeated warnings from his patron that it would jeopardize his financial security, he returned to Norwich in 1824.

Just outside Yarmouth, on the estuary of the Yare, John Crome painted one of his most Dutch-inspired canvases, *Moonrise on the Yare*, which prompted Dawson Turner's remarks on his debt to 'the School of our opposite neighbours upon the Continent' (see Introduction). In his book *Landscape Painting*, John Burnet tells how once, when teaching his pupils on the banks of the Yare, Crome shouted out: 'This is our Academy!'

Haddiscoe, *Norfolk*

The White House (marked by a plaque) on the edge of the village was the home of the Royal Academician Sir John Arnesby Brown and his wife Mia Edwards, a painter

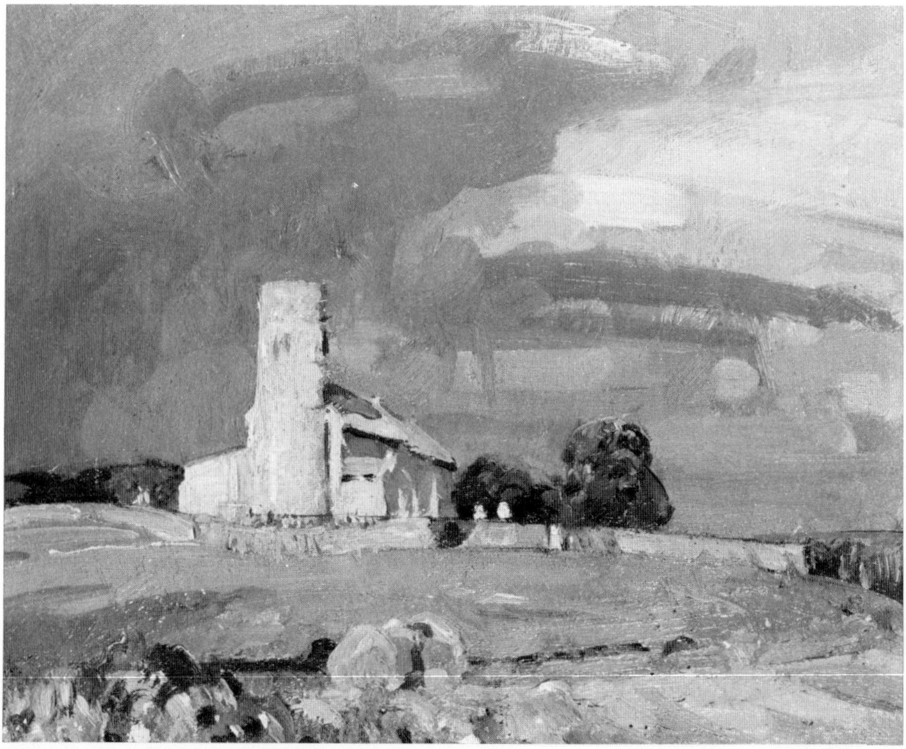

Arnesby Brown
Haddiscoe Church, Norfolk
Oil on panel,
21·6 × 26·9 cm
Castle Museum, Norwich

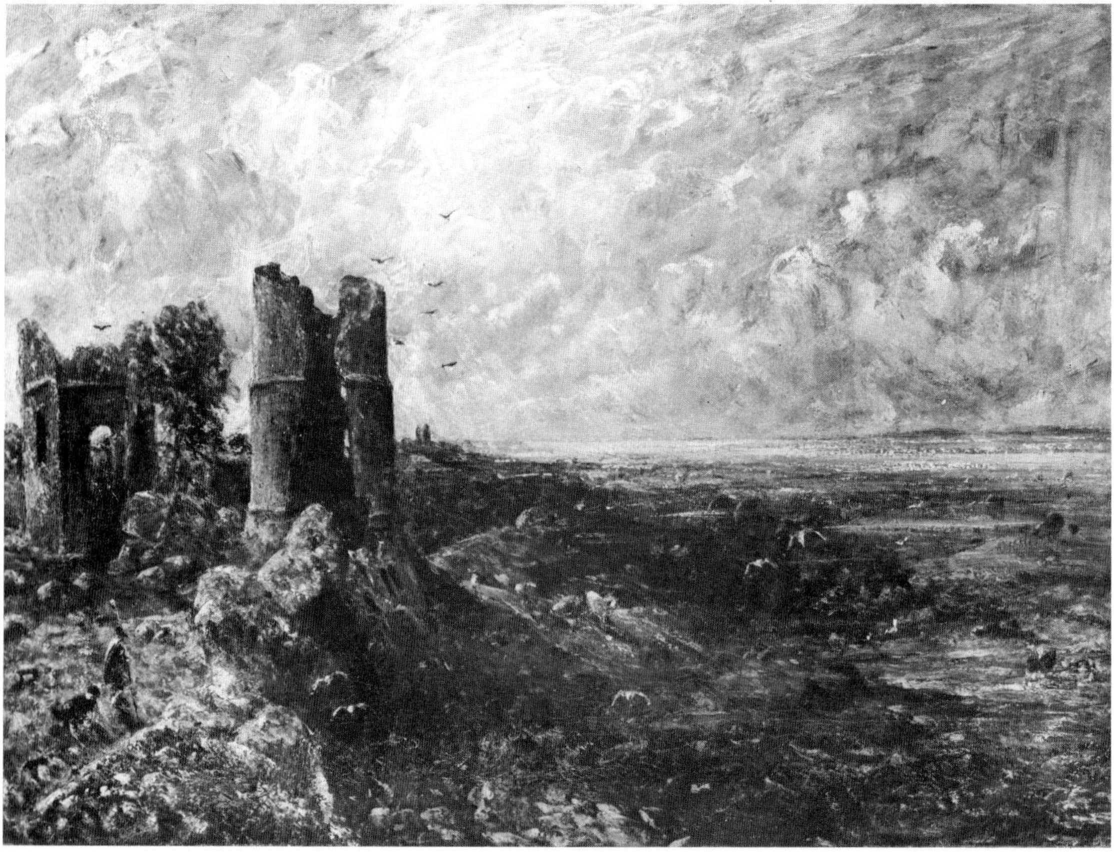

John Constable
Hadleigh Castle
c. 1829: oil on canvas, 123·2 × 167 cm
Tate Gallery, London

of children's portraits. Born in Nottingham in 1866, Brown studied under Hubert von Herkomer at Bushey in Hertfordshire, and shortly afterwards became a prominent member of the Newlyn group of painters in Cornwall. Norfolk was, however, his adopted county, and many of his impressionistic landscapes show the distinctive tower of Haddiscoe Church rising above the surrounding fields.

Hadleigh, *Essex*

John Constable visited Hadleigh in July 1814 and wrote of it to his future wife Maria Bicknell: 'I was always delighted with the melancholy grandeur of a sea shore. At Hadleigh there is the ruin of a castle which from its situation is a really fine place – it commands a view of the Kent hills, the Nore and the North Foreland & looking many miles to sea.' When Maria died in 1828 Constable turned to one of the sketches he had made on that visit fourteen years earlier, as the basis for his *Hadleigh Castle*. The solitary ruin seemed to the artist to embody his personal desolation at that time.

Hadleigh, *Suffolk*

St Mary's Church in Hadleigh is the subject of one of Gainsborough's early paintings, dating from the time he spent in his native Sudbury (q.v.). The work was done for Dr Thomas Tanner, rector of Hadleigh, as an overmantel for his vicarage. It records architectural features of the church which no longer survive, notably the porch, with its large sundial.

Hadleigh was the birthplace of the sculptor Thomas Woolner, who was born in 1825. Woolner, a founder-member of the Pre-Raphaelite Brotherhood, is principally famous for his portrait medallions of famous Victorians such as Lord Tennyson. Apart from a short stay in Australia (his departure for which inspired Ford Madox Brown's well-known painting *The Last of England*, now in Birmingham City Art Gallery), he spent most of his life in London.

Living near Hadleigh, at Benton End, just south of the village on the B1070, is Sir Cedric Morris, Bt. Born in Wales in 1889, Morris tried, among other things, farmwork in Canada and singing at the Royal

Thomas Gainsborough
St Mary's Church, Hadleigh
1748; oil on canvas, 91·4×190·5 cm
Private collection: on loan to Gainsborough's House, Sudbury

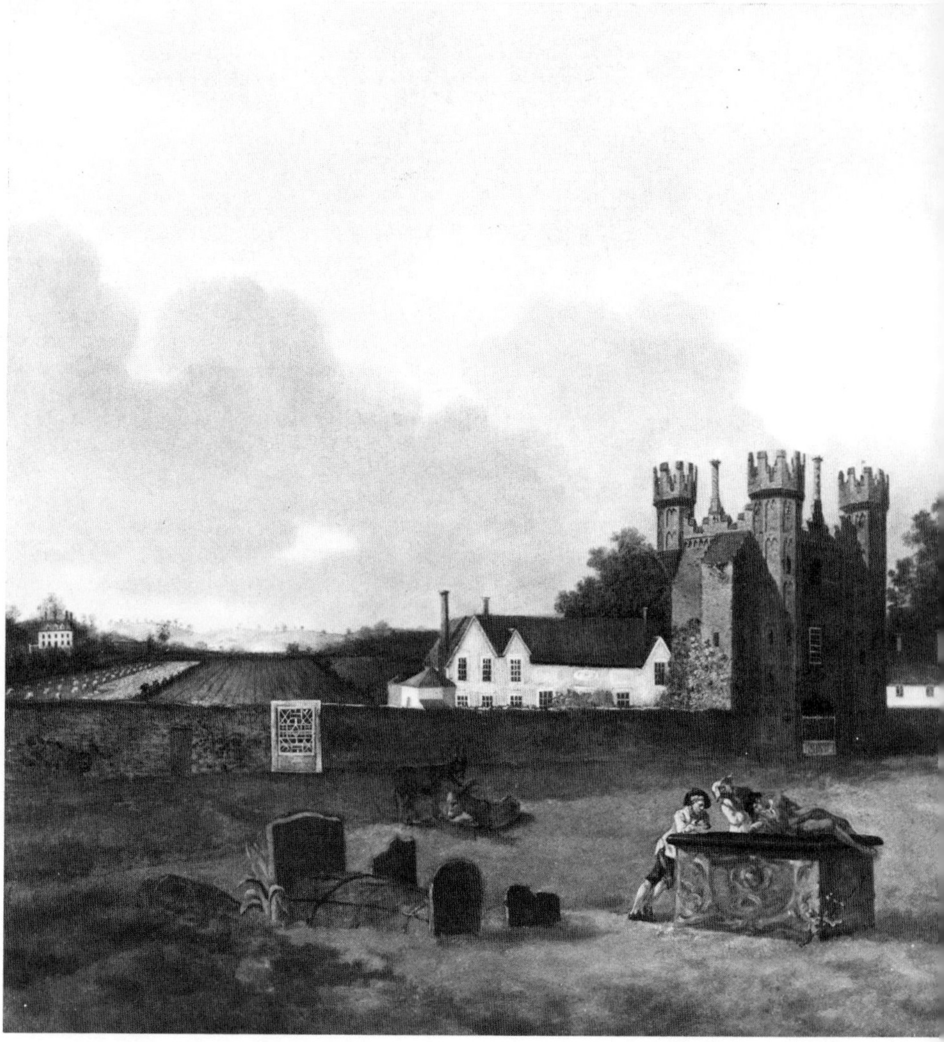

OPPOSITE: Mendham Mills (home of Alfred Munnings)

College of Music in London before finally deciding to become a painter in 1914. He studied for a while at the reactionary Académie Delécluze in Paris, but the First World War put a stop to his formal training. In 1919 he met Arthur Lett-Haines, a painter himself, who remained Morris's companion until his death in 1977. After spending time in Cornwall, Paris and London, where Morris was elected a member of the 'London Group', the two finally settled in East Anglia in the 1930s. Among their contributions to art in this region was the setting up, in 1936, of the East Anglian School of Painting at Dedham, where they then lived, and, ten years later, the Colchester Art Society, of which John Nash (see *Wormingford*) became the President.

The tall, slightly decayed house at Benton End is surrounded by a magnificent garden. Morris is as devoted to gardening as to art, and, travelling all round the world in the company of Lett-Haines, has combined painting trips with searches for exotic botanic specimens to bring back home; these plants are the subject of his most popular canvases, all painted with startlingly vivid colours. Lett-Haines was a very different artist, more eclectic, experimental in media, and concerned with symbolism; a few years before he died he designed a heraldic inn-sign for their local pub, The Red Lion.

Ipswich, *Suffolk*

Thomas Gainsborough lived in Ipswich from 1752 to 1759, working mainly on portrait commissions for local patrons. According to tradition, his first residence here was at 41 Lower Brook Street; by 1753,

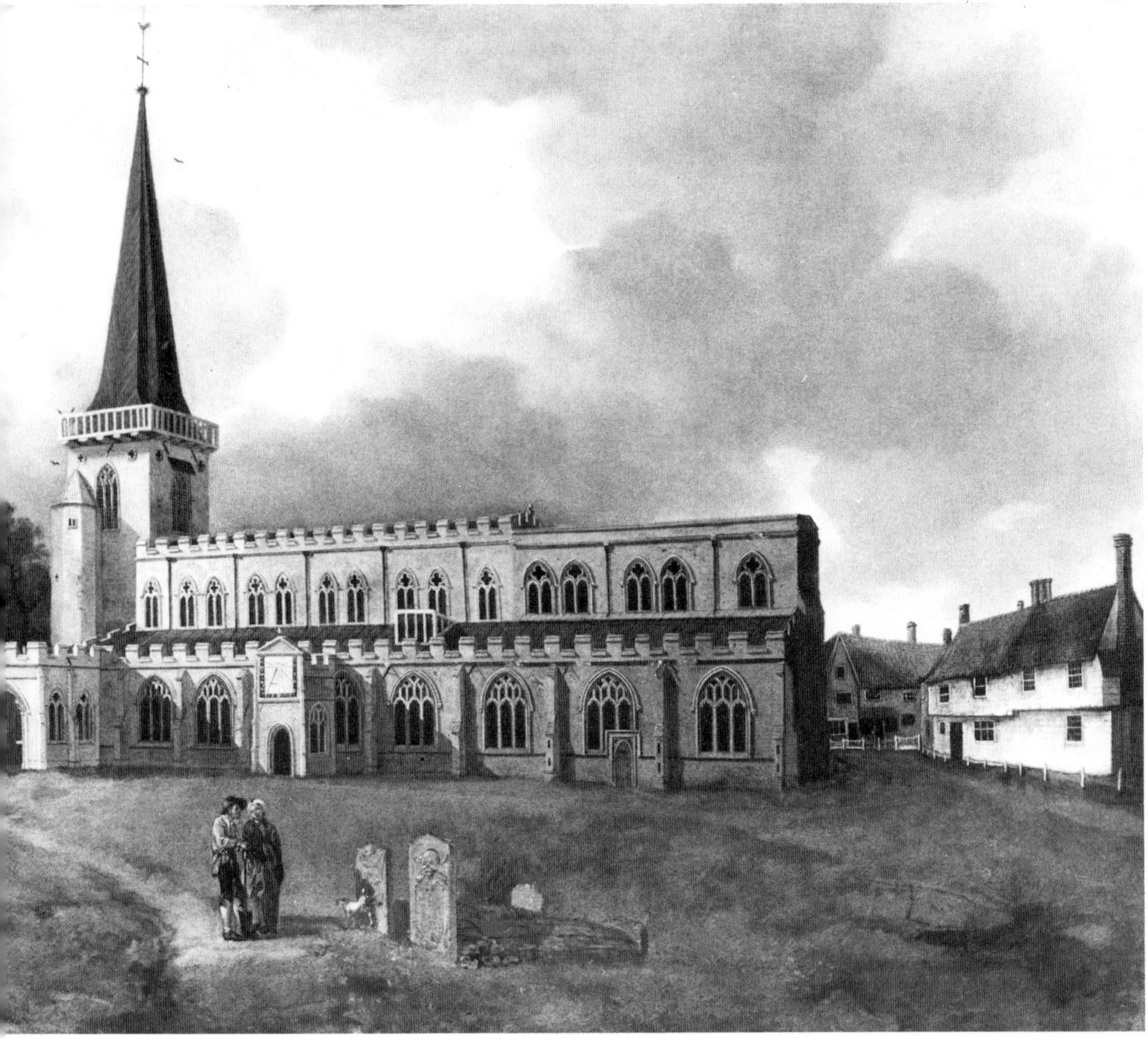

however, he was certainly living opposite the County Gaol, in Foundation Street (both houses have been demolished). Early examples of Gainsborough's Ipswich portraiture show a stiffness in the poses and a detailed handling of paint which by the end of his stay had given way to the more relaxed manner and fluency of technique for which he later became famous.

Mendham, *Suffolk*

Alfred Munnings, the popular painter of horses, grew up at Mendham Mills, of which his father was proprietor. He left home at the age of fourteen to train as a poster-designer in Norwich. But he returned to Mendham after his six-year apprenticeship was over, and set up his first studio in a converted carpenter's shop near the crossroads at the east end of the village.

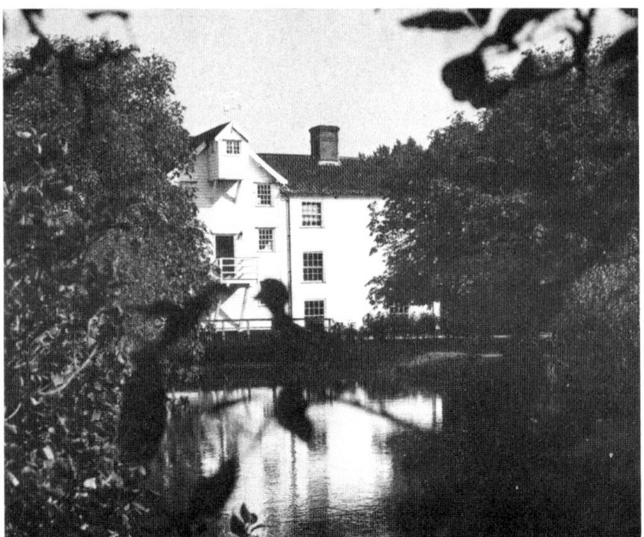

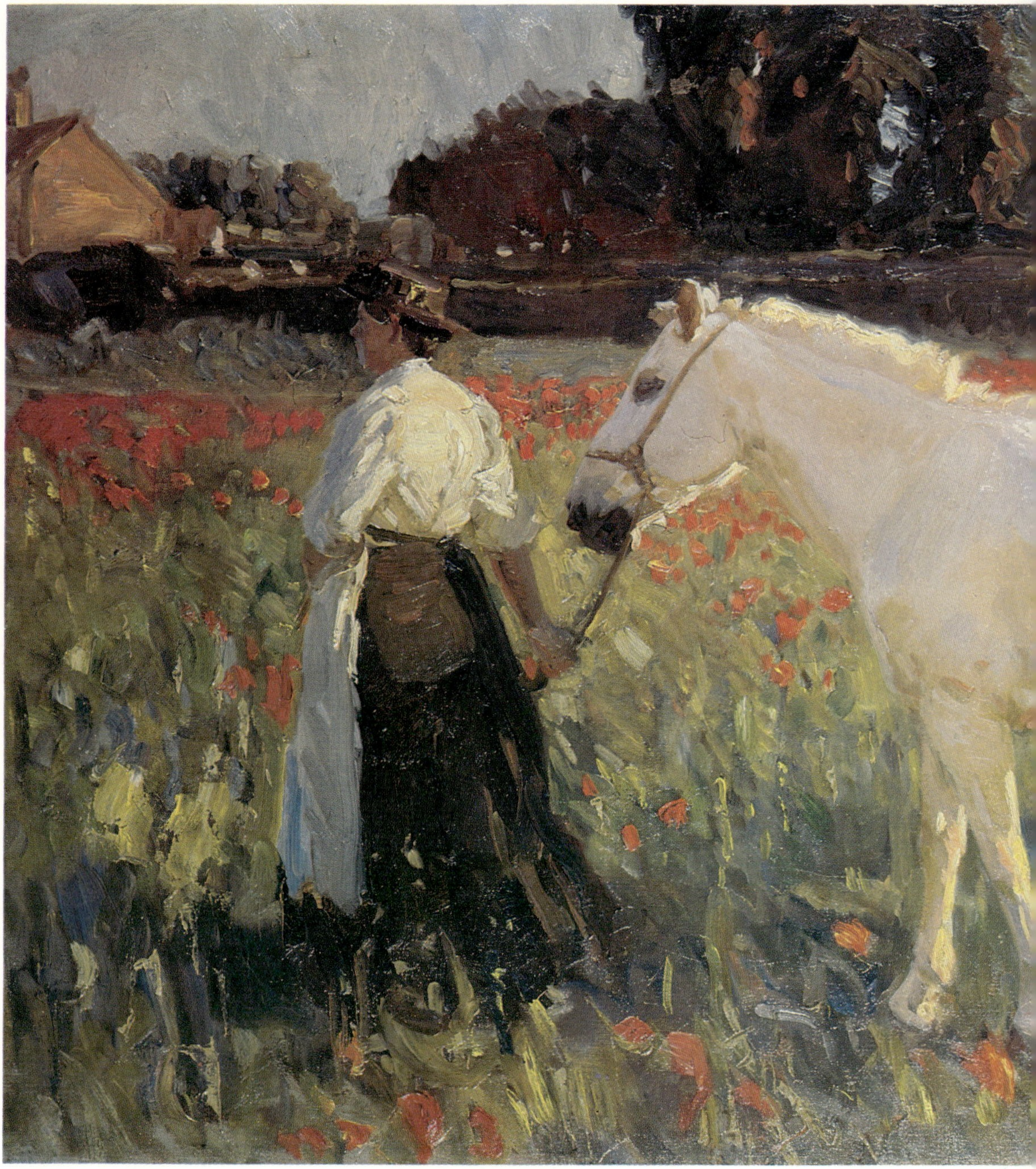

The paintings of Munnings's Mendham period are characterized by a remarkable colouristic and compositional inventiveness. The artist wrote of his *Poppy Field* of 1905–6: 'This was the first real go I had at a large painting, trying to see colour. I remember painting it on one of my father's fields. End of Red Lion Inn on left, and right background – the Churchyard trees at Mendham. Charlotte Grey leading the pony. 3 afternoons' work . . . or 2 . . .'

Newmarket, *Suffolk*

The rubbing-down house, which was one of the most familiar landmarks on Newmarket Heath, features in several works by George Stubbs; but the first artist actually to live at Newmarket (from 1812 to 1825) was Ben Marshall, who was Stubbs's successor as England's leading sporting painter. In this century, the greatest devotee of horse-racing among artists has been Sir Alfred

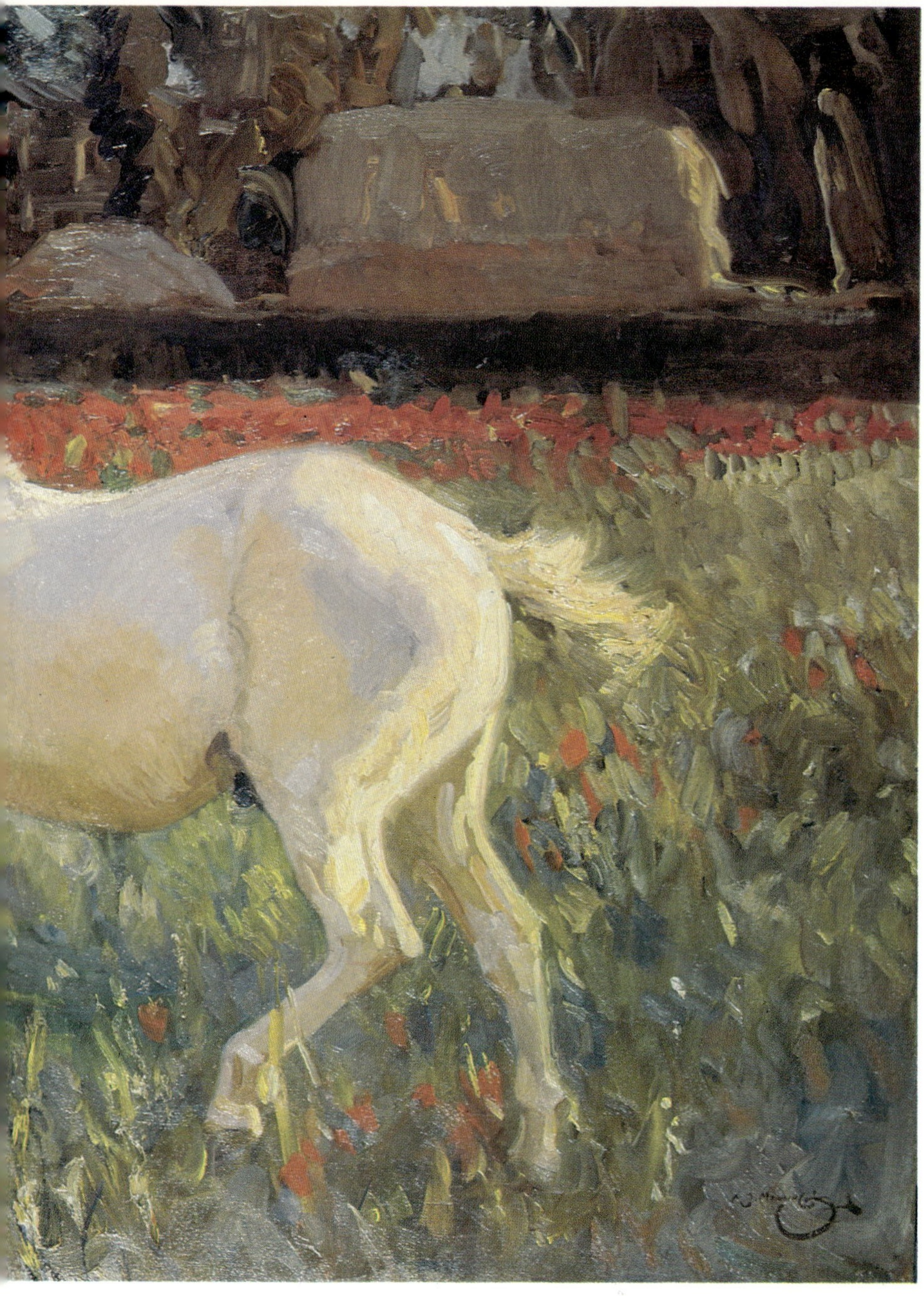

Alfred Munnings
The Poppy Field
1905–6; oil on canvas, 76·2 × 127 cm
Dundee Museums and Art Gallery

Munnings. Munnings painted many Newmarket scenes, most of which were done at the studio he had here in the early 1950s. His favourite subject was the lining up of the horses at the starting post.

Norwich, *Norfolk*

Writing in 1950, Sir Alfred Munnings looked back affectionately at the Norwich he had known in the 1890s: 'Norwich itself was then a beautiful place, and looked almost the same as it must have done in the days of Crome and Cotman. I now realize what a playground it was for the artist. No wonder it had its famous Norwich School of Painters, for the artist is dependent on his environment, and no artists had a more truly picturesque home than this old city of gardens, with its cathedral, its fifty churches, its river with wherries, boats and barges, quays and bridges. There are

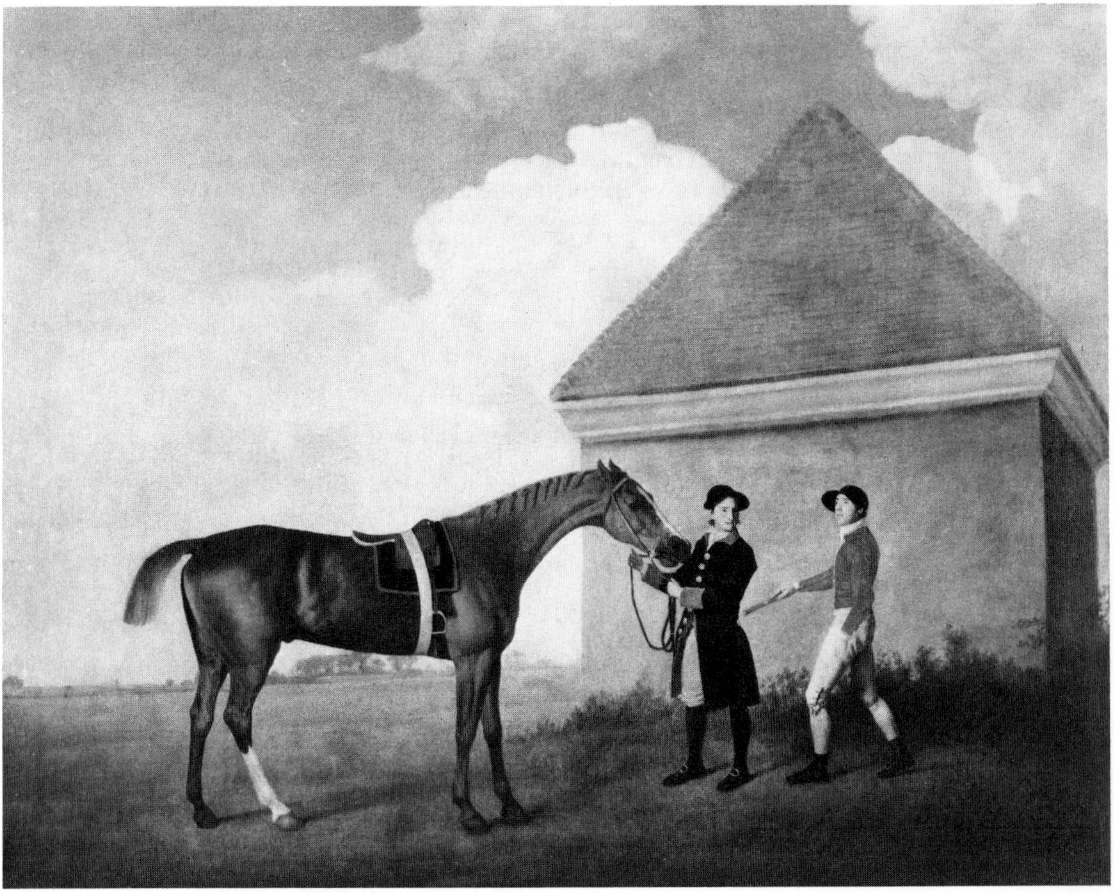

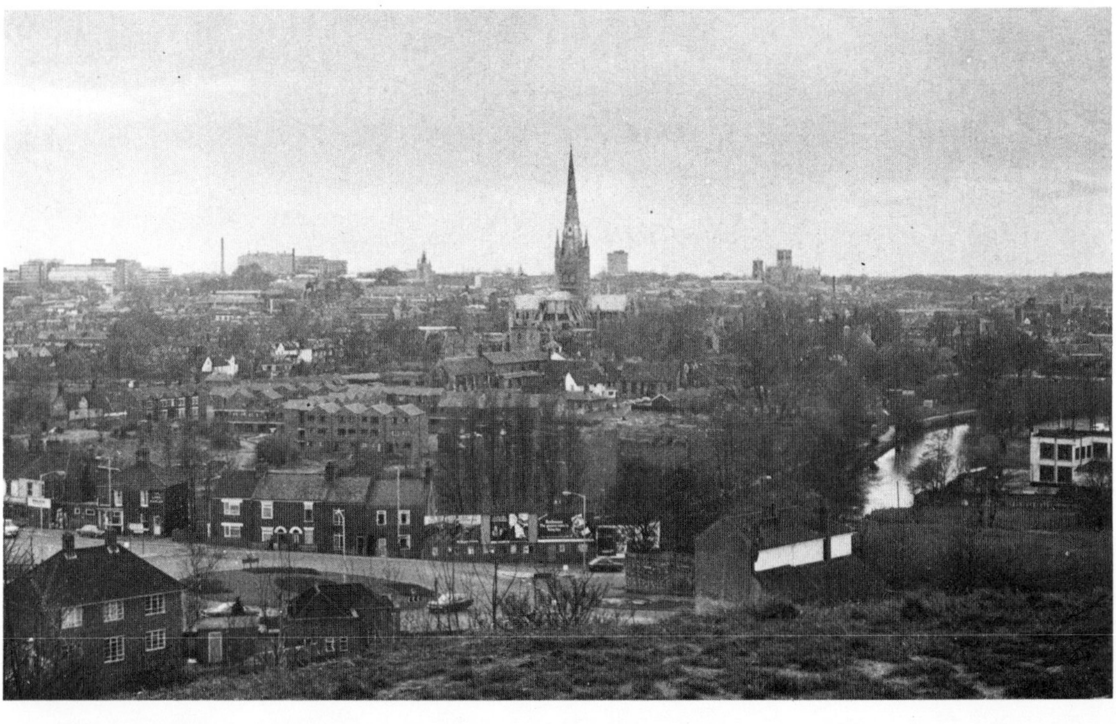

towers on the ancient walls of the city, alleyways leading to courtyards and back streets, with churches hidden away, set in churchyards filled with tombs of parishioners. . . . Such an unlimited wealth of motifs would tempt the dullest painter.'

Norwich did indeed retain its medieval appearance until remarkably late in its history. In 1800 it was still contained almost wholly inside its medieval walls, and even by 1914 it had only extended three-quarters of a mile beyond those limits. Norwich's importance as an art centre dates from the early years of the nineteenth century. In the Norwich Directory of 1783 only one native artist is recorded as working in the city. Ironically enough, its waning prosperity and consequent decline in population, brought on by England's war with France (1793–1815), coincided with an extraordinary rise in the number of local artists. In February 1803 the inaugural meeting of the Norwich Society was held, its purpose being to make an 'Enquiry into the Rise, Progress and Present State of Painting, Architecture and Sculpture, with a view to point out the Best Methods of Study to attain Greater Perfection in these Arts'. The intentions of the Society were to meet regularly to discuss matters concerning art, and, more importantly, to hold an annual exhibition during the August Assizes. The first of these took place in 1805.

All the greatest artists of the Norwich School were associated with the Society, the most notable being John Crome, its traditional founder, and John Sell Cotman. Crome, who was born in 1768, spent almost his entire life in Norwich. His father was a journeyman weaver who also kept an alehouse, The Griffin, in King Street. This was later described by Dawson Turner, the great patron of Crome and Cotman, as 'a public house of far from the highest description'. Crome himself later became a notorious drinker, and his association with pubs extended to painting the signs of at least two of them (The Three Cranes in the Cathedral Close and The Lame Dog on the corner of Queen's Road). It should also be mentioned that the first meetings of the Norwich Society took place in The Hole in the Wall. None of these pubs now survives. Between 1781 and 1783 Crome acted as errand-boy to Dr Edward Rigby, an active-minded medical practitioner, whose house, off St Giles Street, still stands. In 1785 he became an apprentice to F. Whistler, a coach- and sign-painter who lived sixty yards from Dr Rigby at No. 55 St Giles Street. It seems that Crome was a late starter as an artist, producing his first sketch in oil only in 1790, when he was twenty-two. By 1798 he had already started giving private drawing lessons; in 1811 he became drawing-master at Miss Heazel's

OVERLEAF:
John Sell Cotman
Mousehold Heath, Norwich
c. 1810; pencil and watercolour, 30·3 × 46·4 cm
Castle Museum, Norwich

OPPOSITE, ABOVE:
George Stubbs
Eclipse
1770; oil on canvas, 100·5 × 132 cm
Jockey Club, Newmarket

OPPOSITE, BELOW:
Recent photograph of Norwich from Mousehold Heath

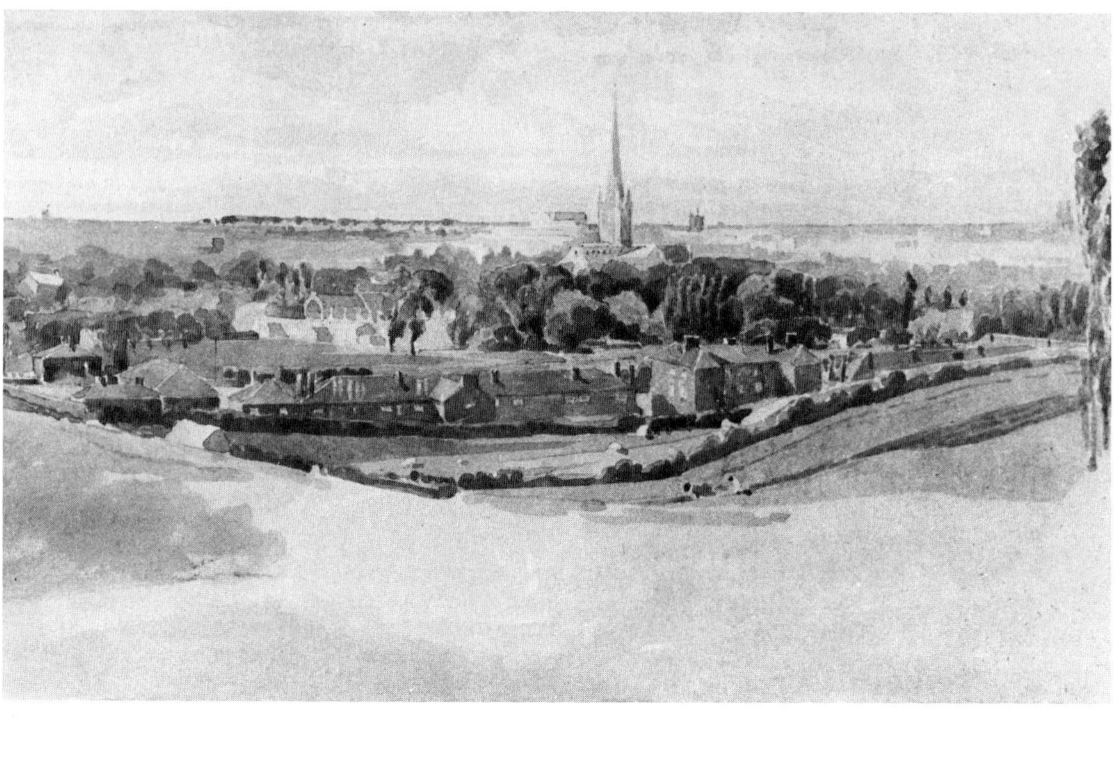

John Thirtle
Norwich from Mousehold Heath (detail)
Pencil and watercolour
Castle Museum, Norwich

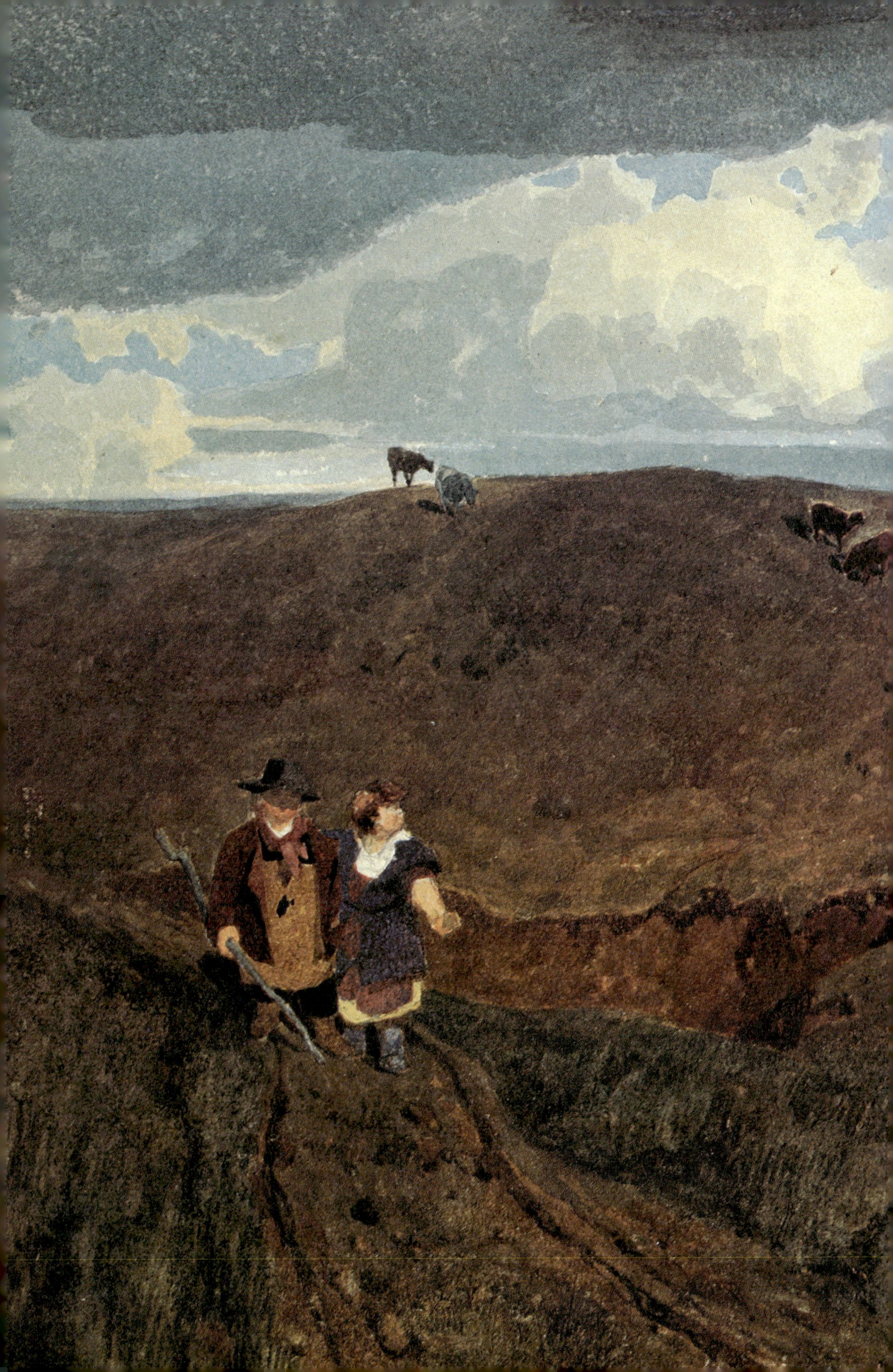

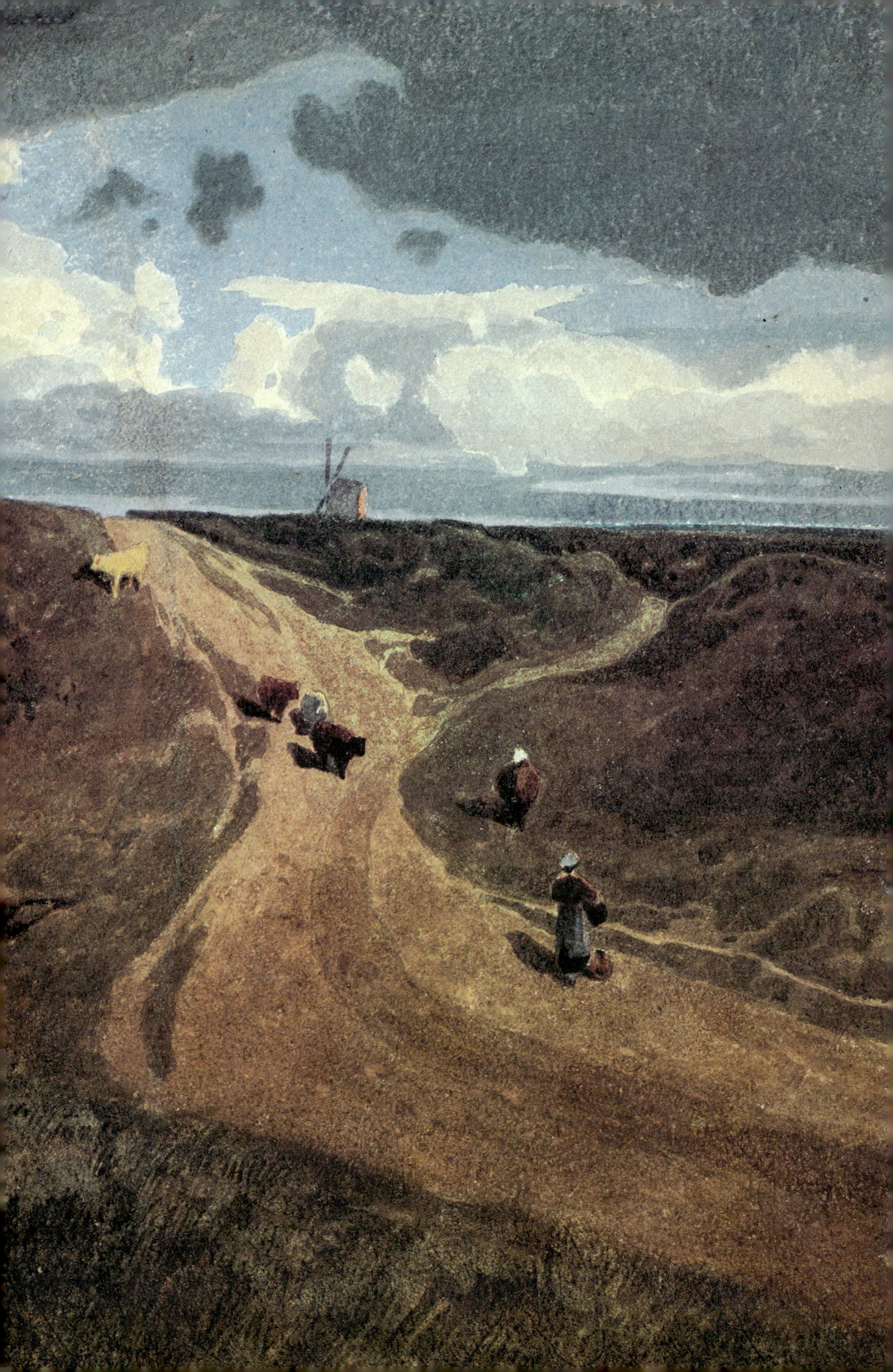

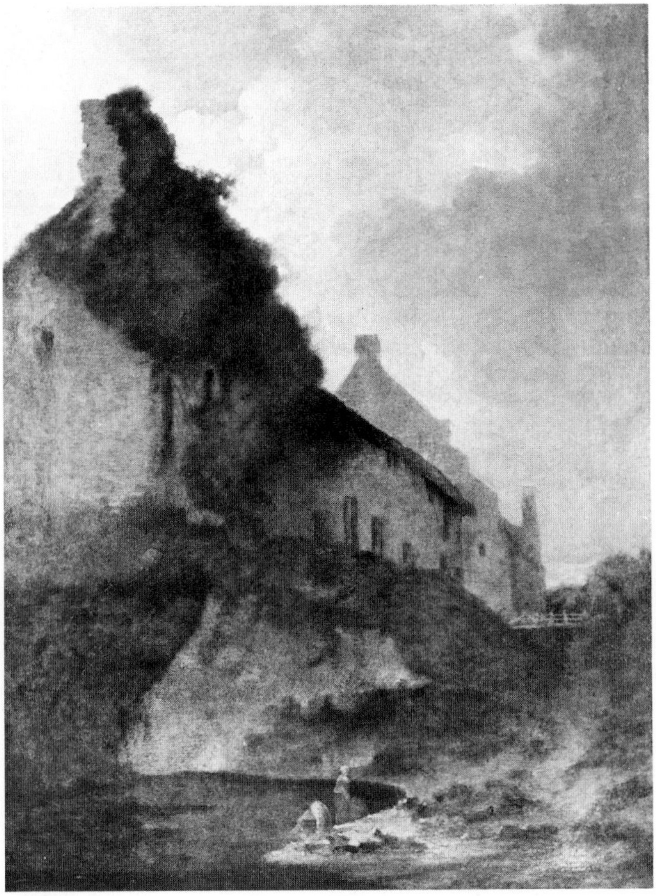

John Crome
Carrow Abbey, Norwich
c. 1805; oil on canvas, 133·7×99 cm
Castle Museum, Norwich

OPPOSITE, ABOVE:
John Sell Cotman
St Luke's Chapel, Norwich Cathedral
1808; pencil and watercolour, 35·2×46·1 cm
Castle Museum, Norwich

BELOW:
John Sell Cotman
From my Father's House at Thorpe
1842; oil on canvas, 68·6×94 cm
Castle Museum, Norwich

Seminary at Norwich, and in 1813 held the same appointment at Norwich Grammar School. To teach art was the most lucrative occupation for a provincial painter, and Crome undoubtedly dominated the market in Norwich. Unlike Cotman, he was a business-minded man, who managed to prosper financially. By 1802 he had already moved into his double-fronted house at 17 Gildengate Street, now St George's Street (the whole area has been completely altered by a flyover and H.M. Stationery Office), where he lived until his death in 1821. He is buried in the church of St George's, Tombland.

After Crome's death, his family – six of his children also became painters – suffered increasing financial hardship. This greatly pleased Cotman, who, on his appointment as Professor of Drawing at King's College, London, wrote to Dawson Turner: 'my oft-told dream terminated with the success of myself and my family and the downfall of the family of Crome.' As a personality, Cotman was in every respect the opposite of Crome – exceedingly difficult, introverted, subject to fits of extreme depression, financially foolhardy and constantly dissatisfied. Born in 1782, he was the son of a barber's assistant living at 26 Bridge Street, St George's (gone). From the start Cotman wanted to make an impression in London circles, and despised the purely provincial aspirations of an artist such as Crome. Ironically, when his ambitions were thwarted and he was forced to make his living as a drawing-master, he found the market already overcrowded. In 1798 he moved to London, and between then and 1807 he divided his time between London, Yorkshire (where many of his greatest watercolours were done) and Norwich, which he visited every summer to stay a short period with his parents.

Cotman missed the first two exhibitions of the Norwich Society, and when he first exhibited there, in 1807, he arrogantly assumed that his work would be conspicuous among that of his stay-at-home colleagues in Norfolk, and that he would attract a much wider market. To emphasize his uniqueness he decided not to compete as a painter of local scenery, but instead to develop a line in portraiture, not the strong point of the Norwich School. He soon abandoned the idea. After a long period in Yarmouth (1812–23; see *Great Yarmouth*) he bought, on his return to Norwich, an enormous house at St Martin's-at-Palace-Gate (plaque). Dawson Turner considered that he was paying 'too large a rent for too big a place'. Cotman looked for other accommodation, but his uncompromising nature eventually led to his complete refusal to change address. Until his move to London in 1835, Cotman's last years were spent on the verge of penury and madness. In 1831 he became Vice-President of the Norwich Society, and in 1833 its President; when he eventually left Norwich the Society came to an end. As with Crome, most of his children became artists (the most famous being Miles Edmund), but they also seem to have inherited their father's mental instability, and the later history of Cotman's family is just as depressing as that of his rival's.

Crome and Cotman were very different artists, even in the media they used, the former devoting himself largely to oils, and the latter to watercolour. The bluntness of Crome's character is reflected in his art. His approach to nature was a spontaneous one, and the crudity of his technique (his excessive use of bitumen has caused an appalling deterioration of his works) resulted in art of at times primitive forcefulness. In later life his paintings did,

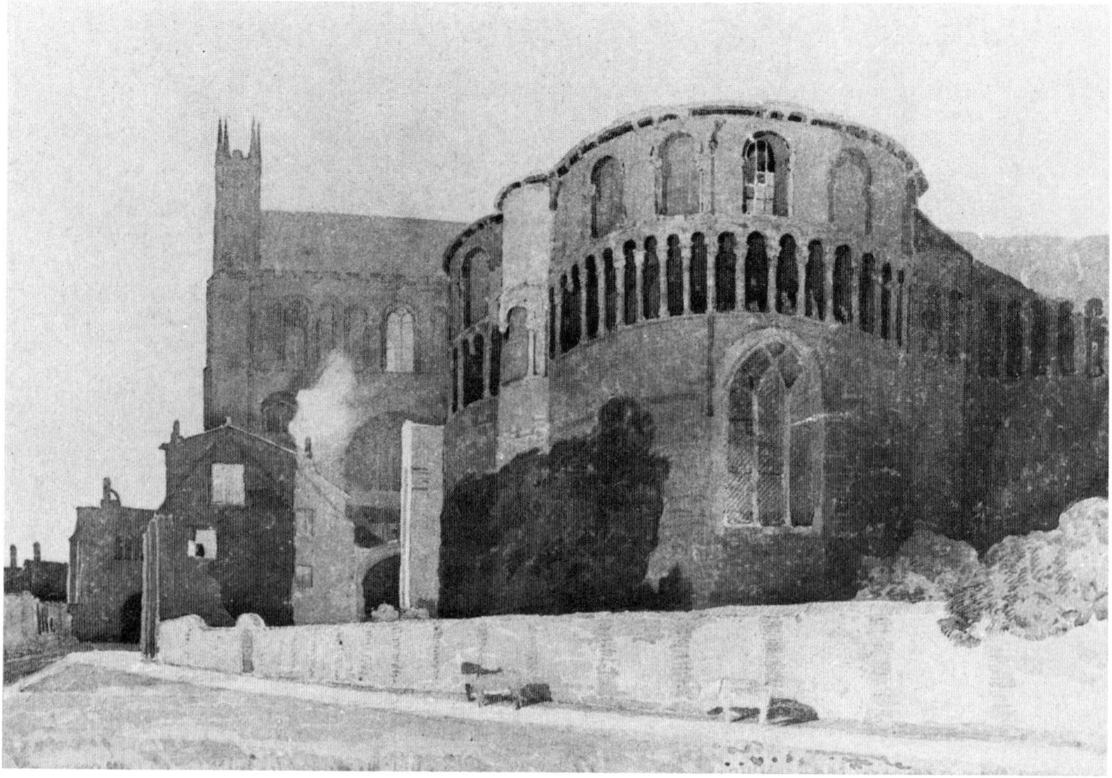

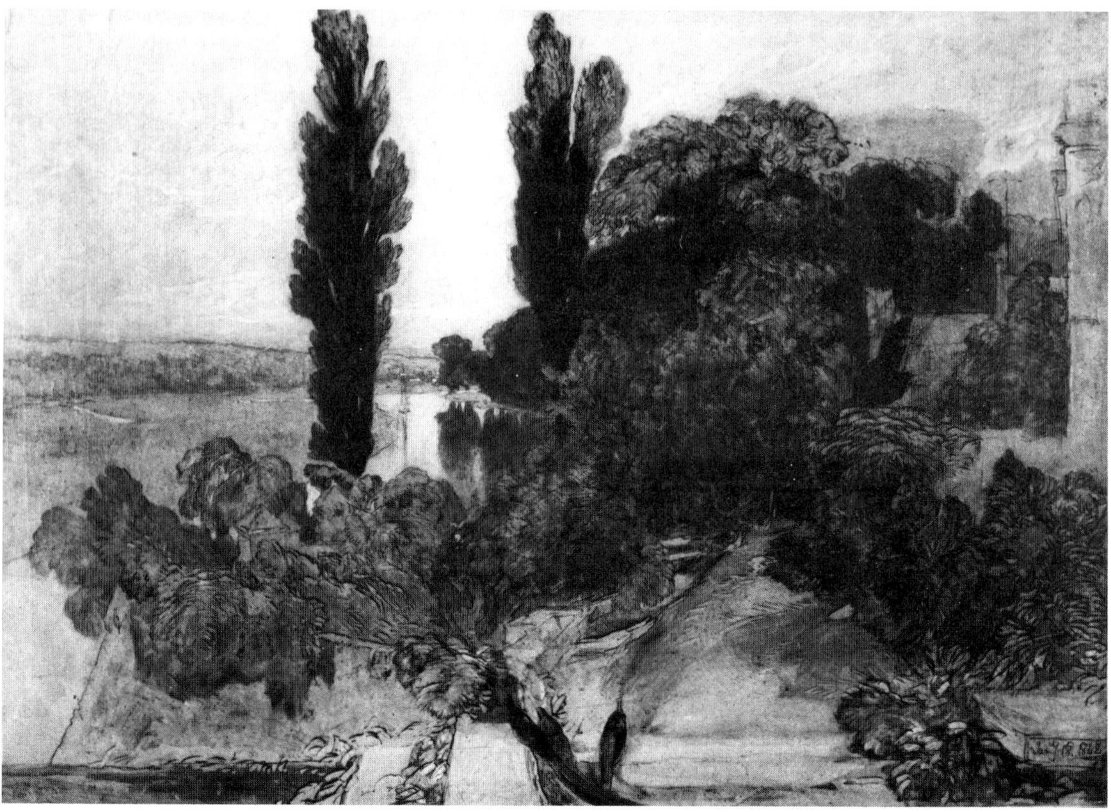

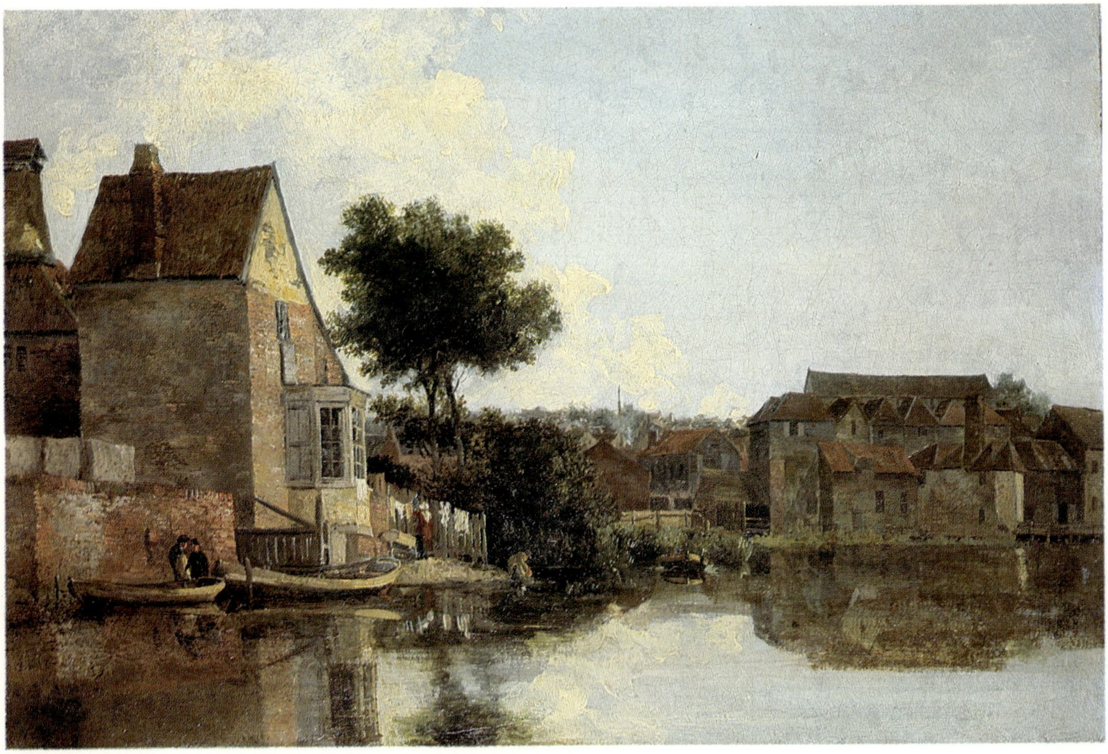

John Crome
Back of the New Mills (detail)
Oil on canvas, 41·3 × 54 cm
Castle Museum, Norwich

however, acquire a greater finish, with brighter, more conventional colours. Cotman's greatness, on the other hand, lay in his ability to reduce nature to strikingly simple and delicate patterns. It is easy to understand how this more structured and precious approach appealed less to orthodox taste than the highly accessible works of Crome.

Other important artists associated with the Norwich School include Cotman's brother-in-law John Thirtle, Robert Ladbrooke, James Stark (a pupil of Crome), the Reverend E. Daniell, Henry Ninham, Joseph Stannard (a pupil of Ladbrooke), George Vincent, Thomas Lound, and Henry Bright.

Two distinguished outsiders who spent a period in Norwich were the portraitists Sir William Beechey and John Opie. Beechey, an Oxfordshire man, was initially apprenticed to a lawyer, but later ran away to become a sign-painter in Norwich, and eventually went to the Royal Academy Schools in London. By 1783 he was a part-time resident in Norwich, living at 4 Market Place (gone). Like many London portraitists he maintained a provincial connection to keep himself occupied when his clientèle was out of town. In 1793 he married, as his second wife, a Norwich miniaturist, Phyllis Anne Jessup. Beechey had a considerable influence on Crome, and described him as 'a very awkward, uninformed country lad, but extremely shrewd in all his remarks upon art, though he wanted words to express his meaning'. Crome was also an acquaintance of Opie, who painted a very striking portrait of him. Opie paid his first visit to Norwich in 1797, when he met and married the beautiful novelist Amelia Alderson. From that date he regularly spent time in the city. In 1798, when Cotman was considering becoming an artist, Opie was asked for an opinion of his work. This was not encouraging: 'Let him rather black boots than follow the profession of artist.'

The most generally painted parts of Norwich were not the major historical monuments such as the cathedral and the castle but rather the less important, more dilapidated medieval buildings. Virtually all the Norwich artists depicted such relics of the city's past as the Cow Tower and the Devil's Tower, both of which survive. Across the river from the Devil's Tower are the ruins of Carrow Abbey, now in the grounds of Colman's factory; these were painted by Crome about 1805, in a work with dark, brutal and primitive qualities that make it one of the masterpieces of his early maturity. Most of the medieval city has now gone, however. Such decayed areas as the New Mills, which inspired two of the greatest paintings of Crome's later years, have now given way to modern developments.

The best view of the city is to be had from Mousehold Heath. From here, in the words of George Borrow in *Lavengro* (1851), 'the eye beholds a scene which cannot fail to awaken, even in the least sensitive bosom, feelings of pleasure and admiration.' The view is recorded in a finely detailed and sweeping panorama by Thirtle and in an oil by Sir John Arnesby Brown (both in the Norwich Castle Museum). Mousehold Heath was a favourite place of Crome's, and his many paintings and etchings of the heath are characterized by a distinctive windmill, which was pulled down in the 1930s. One evening, when Cotman was walking on the heath, he saw the sun setting behind a ruined building on the hill in front of him. He made an instant pencil-jotting, and noted the colours: this resulted in a watercolour now in the Norwich Castle Museum.

On the outskirts of Norwich, another of the popular sites for artists was the elegant village of Thorpe, on the River Yare. In 1836 one writer referred to 'this Richmond of Norfolk' as being generally considered 'one of the most charming inner summer retreats in the kingdom'. Now the village has become a suburb of Norwich; even in 1954 Sir Alfred Munnings, who lived there during his last two years at art school, could write that 'shades of Crome and Cotman might well sigh around the approaches of Thorpe. . . . In the eighteen nineties Thorpe Gardens were all that one could imagine such a place to have been in the days of Stannard and Thirtle. I can think of nothing more holiday-like or carefree than they looked, with their boats and riverside lawn and frontage.' Many of the village's elegant mansions still survive, however, and so does the semi-detached cottage to which Cotman's father retired. A late watercolour of Cotman's entitled *From my Father's House at Thorpe* is an essay in nostalgia, the real site having been transformed in the imagination, with peacocks on the lawn and an aura of Italy. Also part fact and part fiction is Stannard's *Thorpe Water Frolic*. The Frolic, or boat-race, was instigated by the industrialist John Harvey, and became a notable public holiday, attracting in 1825, the year of Stannard's imaginative recreation of the event, an estimated 20,000 spectators. In the picture Harvey is shown on a gondola; no doubt he saw the event in terms of one of the Venetian regattas he had seen. Stannard's interest was more than just aesthetic and social, for he was also a skilled oarsman and owned a prize-winnning boat, the *Cytherea*.

The Thorpe Water Frolic replaced the

Joseph Stannard
Thorpe Water Frolic (detail)
c. 1825; oil on canvas, 108 × 172·7 cm
Castle Museum, Norwich

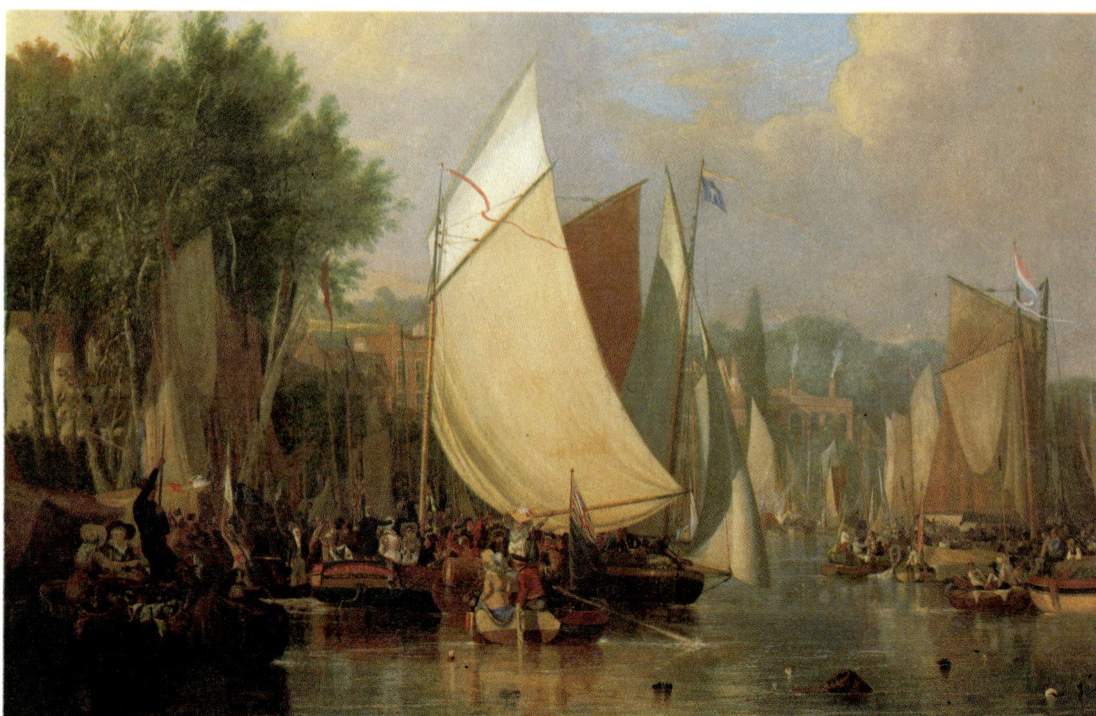

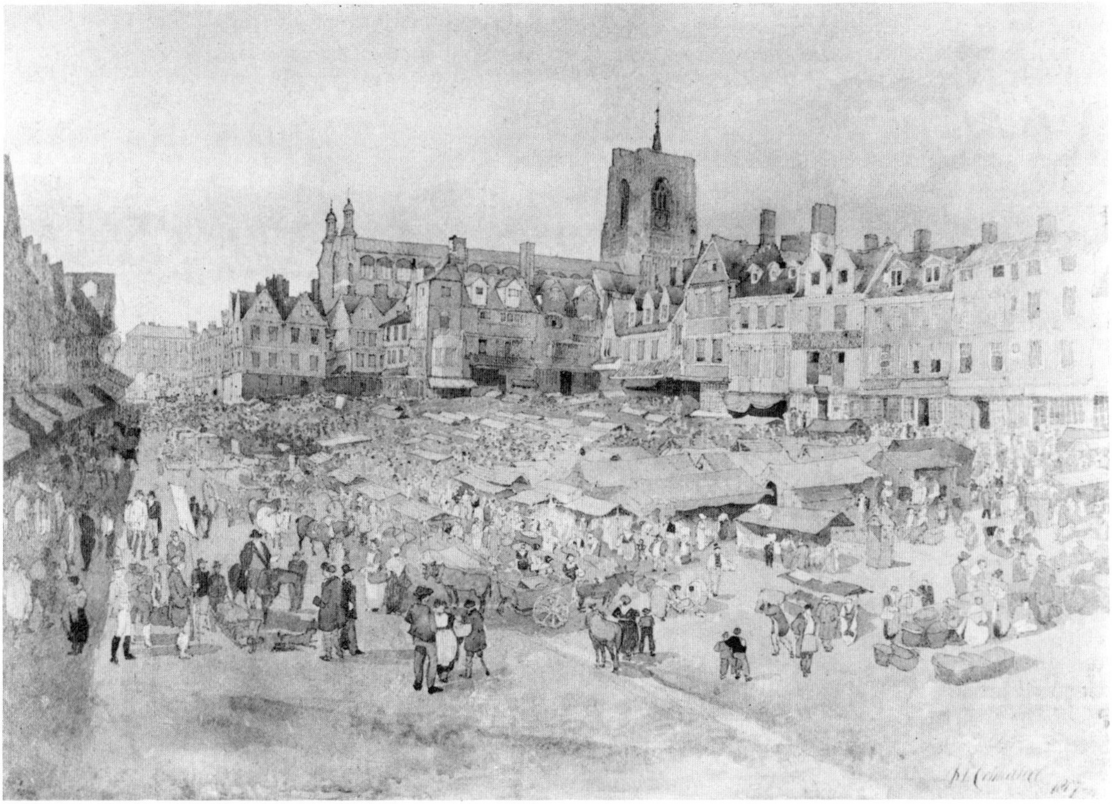

John Sell Cotman
Norwich Market Place
1807; pencil and watercolour, 35·6 × 55·9 cm
Abbot Hall Art Gallery, Kendal

annual river procession from Norwich to Postwick Grove on the River Bure. Postwick Grove was itself a favourite spot for artists, and an oil-sketch of the site by Crome in the Norwich Castle Museum has something of the immediacy, and balance of tonal values, of a Corot.

Also near Norwich was Costessey Park (now in ruins), the home of the Jerningham family, one of the few aristocratic families in Norfolk to show an interest in local art. Many artists were allowed to sketch in the beautiful grounds of their house, and the park is mentioned in John Burnet's *Progress*

Henry Bright
St Benet's Abbey
c. 1847; oil on canvas, 80·3 × 132·9 cm
Castle Museum, Norwich

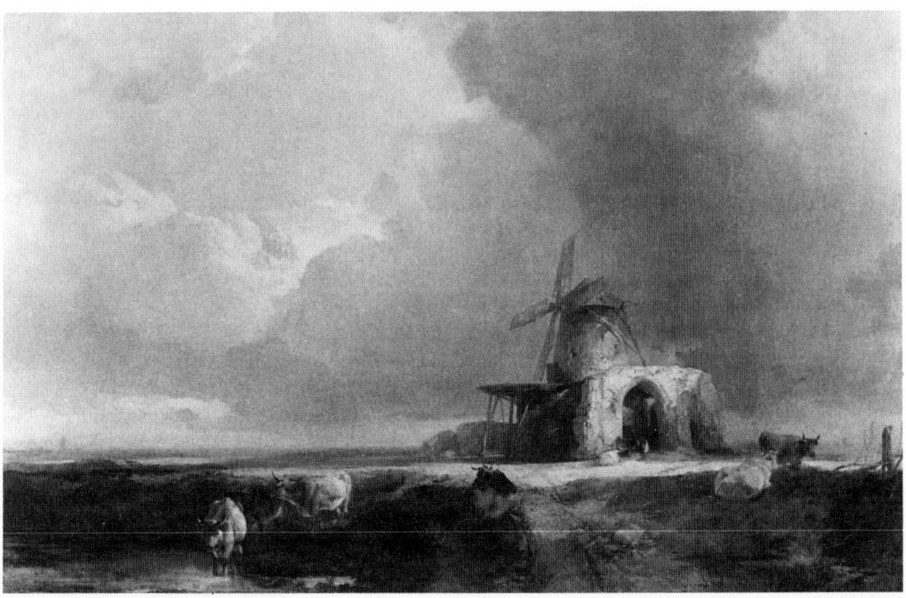

of a Painter (1854), which includes a story about a fictitious painter called Churchill. Churchill was clearly meant as Crome, who used to give drawing-lessons to the Jerningham daughters. A very different sort of patron from the Jerninghams was Thomas Harvey, a master weaver and man of property, who lived at Catton Hall, two miles from the city. While apprenticed to a sign-painter, Crome spent a lot of his time here, studying and copying Harvey's impressive collection of both old and modern masters. It was here that he first came across the work of such Dutch artists as Hobbema and Cuyp, as well as that of more recent, British painters such as Richard Wilson and Gainsborough, the latter being another of Harvey's protégés. A famous painting by Gainsborough hung in the collection, and Dawson Turner emphasized how strongly Crome's *Cottage at Hunstanton* reflected his careful study of it, 'in tone and colour, and handling, and surface'. It was also at Catton Hall that Crome met Sir William Beechey, who gave considerable encouragement to the young artist.

St Benet's Abbey, *Norfolk*

The ruins of the medieval St Benet's Abbey, picturesquely combined with a later windmill, have attracted most of the artists who have worked in East Anglia. Their romantic isolation was captured in one of the best-known paintings of Henry Bright. Bright is always regarded as the last of the Dutch-inspired Norwich School, and his dramatic canvases have much in common with those of Ruisdael.

The further dilapidation of St Benet's in recent times, which has resulted in the disappearance of the windmill's sails, has made it lose much of its grandeur. None the less, it inspired the Royal Academician Edward Seago, whose life was intimately connected with East Anglia. Like Bright, Seago dramatizes the abbey by means of meteorological effects. He was a vivid colourist, influenced by the Impressionists,

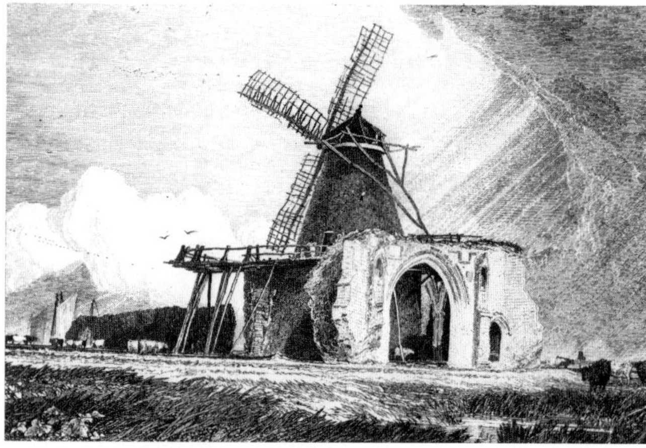

John Sell Cotman
St Benet's Abbey
1813; etching, 34 × 48 cm
Castle Museum, Norwich

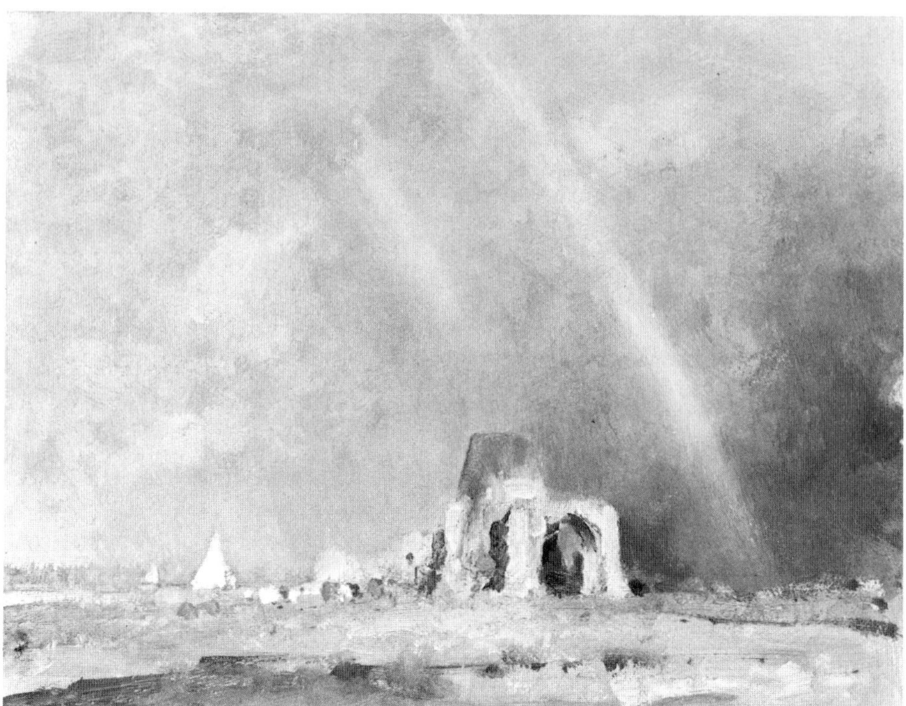

Edward Seago
The Rainbow, St Benet's Abbey
Oil on board, 25·6 × 35·5 cm
Seago Estate

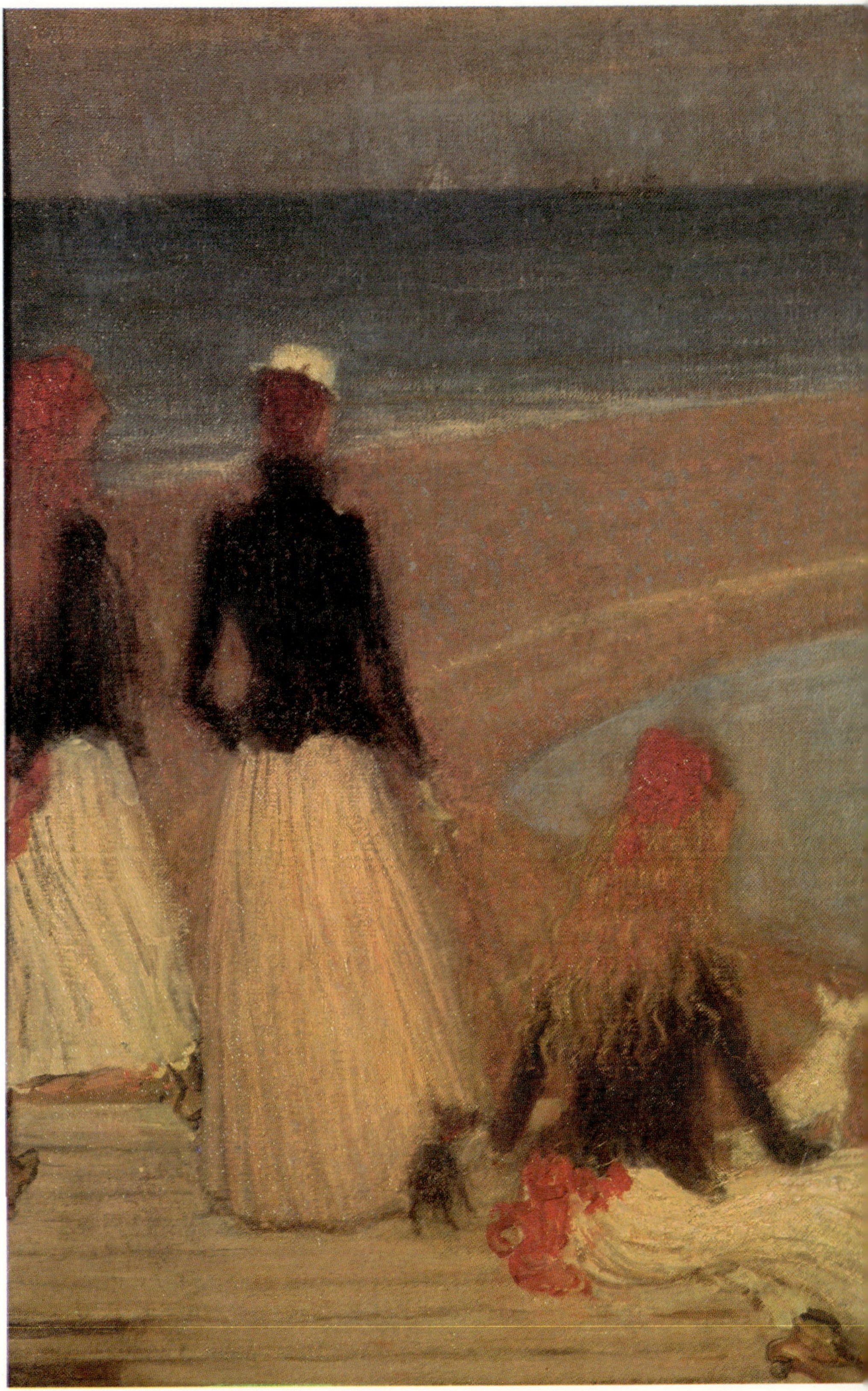

Philip Wilson Steer
The Beach at Walberswick
c. 1889; oil on canvas, 60·2 × 76·2 cm
Tate Gallery, London

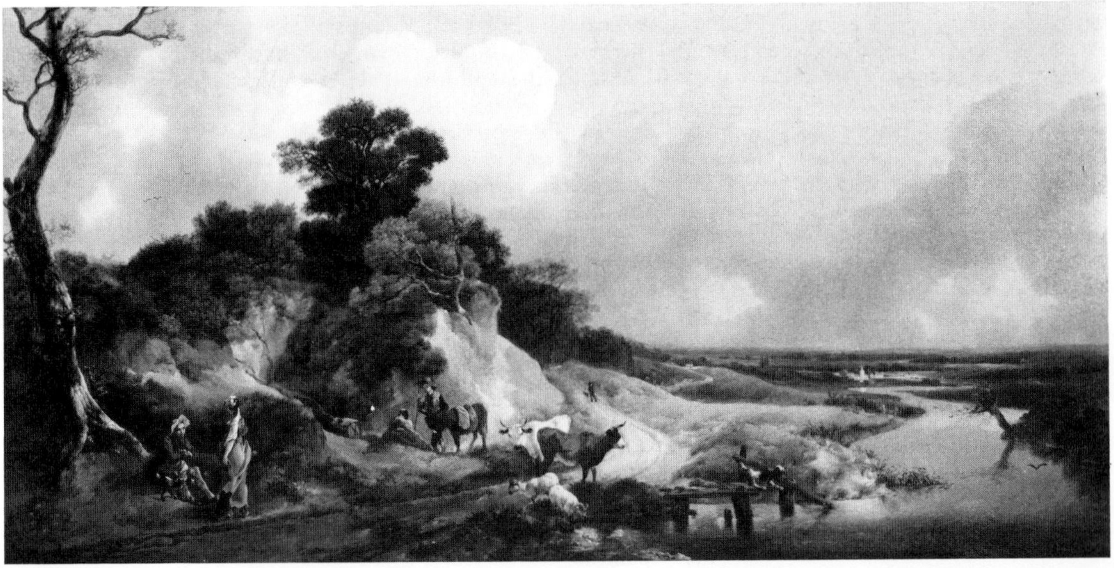

Thomas Gainsborough
Landscape with distant view of Cornard Village
c. 1750; oil on canvas, 76·2 × 151 cm
National Gallery of Scotland, Edinburgh

Charles Rennie Mackintosh
Walberswick
1914; watercolour, 28 × 38·2 cm
Private collection

and characteristically replaces Bright's thunderstorm with a brilliant rainbow.

Sudbury, *Suffolk*

Thomas Gainsborough was the son of a Sudbury wool-weaver. He was born in what is now called Gainsborough Street, in a house distinguished by an elegant façade which was actually added by his father; the house is today open to the public and contains numerous examples of his work. After an unremarkable career at the local grammar school – the headmaster of which was his uncle, Henry Burrough – Gainsborough was sent to London, where he studied and worked as an artist from 1740 to 1748. He then returned to Sudbury, taking lodgings in Friar Street. Commissions were evidently hard to come by in his native town, however, and in 1752 he moved again to Ipswich (q.v.).

Certain paintings which date from Gainsborough's short period of work in Sudbury show identifiable sites in the vicinity. The couple who are the subjects of one of his most famous portraits, *Mr and Mrs Robert Andrews*, lived at Auberies, just outside Sudbury. The background in the work shows the Auberies estate from a point near the south-eastern corner of the house. Gainsborough also painted pure landscapes at this time, often in and around nearby Cornard. The site of the *Landscape with a Distant View of Cornard Village* is difficult to locate specifically, but the village church is certainly recognizable in the background.

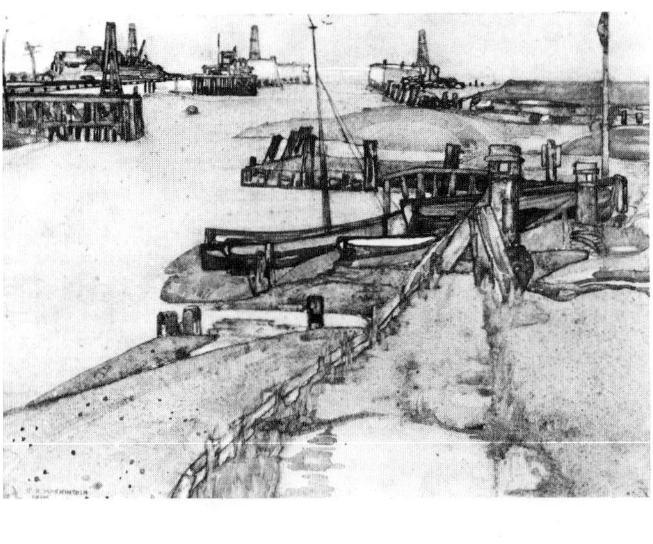

Walberswick, *Suffolk*

The illustrator Charles Keene, famous for his work in *Punch*, was brought up largely in Ipswich and always retained a great affection for Suffolk. In the 1870s he did much drawing along the coast between Dunwich and Southwold, and the old jetty at Walberswick (now a ruin alongside a concrete pier) features in several sketches and cartoons.

In the following decade this small fishing-village became a thriving artistic colony and, most notably, it inspired the greatest works of Philip Wilson Steer. Steer first came to Walberswick in 1884, having spent two years studying art in Paris, and returned almost every summer until 1891. On his earlier visits he probably stayed at an inn on the village green that has since been converted into a private house; later he lodged at Valley Farm in the north-eastern corner of the village.

On the beaches at Walberswick and on the jetty Steer observed dazzling light-effects, translating them into busy, glittering brushwork. Virtually all Steer's Walberswick scenes include groups of colourfully dressed girls, bathing, playing games, or simply looking out to sea. One of these can actually be identified as a local fisherman's daughter, later referred to as Mrs Dolly Brown, who is characteristically shown wearing a white or pink dress, black stockings and a red sash.

In 1914–15 the innovatory Glaswegian architect Charles Rennie Mackintosh and his wife spent some time in Walberswick. After failing to receive any commissions in London, Mackintosh found that the move to Suffolk provided a much needed rest. For the first time in his life he could concentrate entirely on his watercolours, and he produced a series of over thirty flower-studies intended for publication. The beautiful stylization of these does not detract from their botanical accuracy, and many are now housed in the Botany Department at Glasgow University. During the day the Mackintoshes worked in a studio down by the river, and in the evening went for long walks in the country. Their wanderings aroused local suspicion during this tense period at the outbreak of the First World War. When a military inspection revealed letters from the Viennese Secessionists (an Austrian group of artists), the conclusion was inevitable: they were enemy agents. After they were cleared, they moved back to the safer surroundings of Chelsea.

Wormingford, *Essex*

In the Stour Valley, just outside Wormingford, stands Bottengols, the cottage where John Nash spent the last thirty-four years of his life. John, like his elder and more famous brother Paul, was one of the most significant influences on British landscape painting this century. His first important introduction to East Anglia was in 1912, when he went on a walking tour along the Norfolk coast with a Slade friend of Paul's, Claughton Pellew-Harvey. For Nash, who had received no formal training as an artist, Pellew-Harvey's advice on painting proved invaluable, and in the following year he had his first exhibition in London. Nash and his

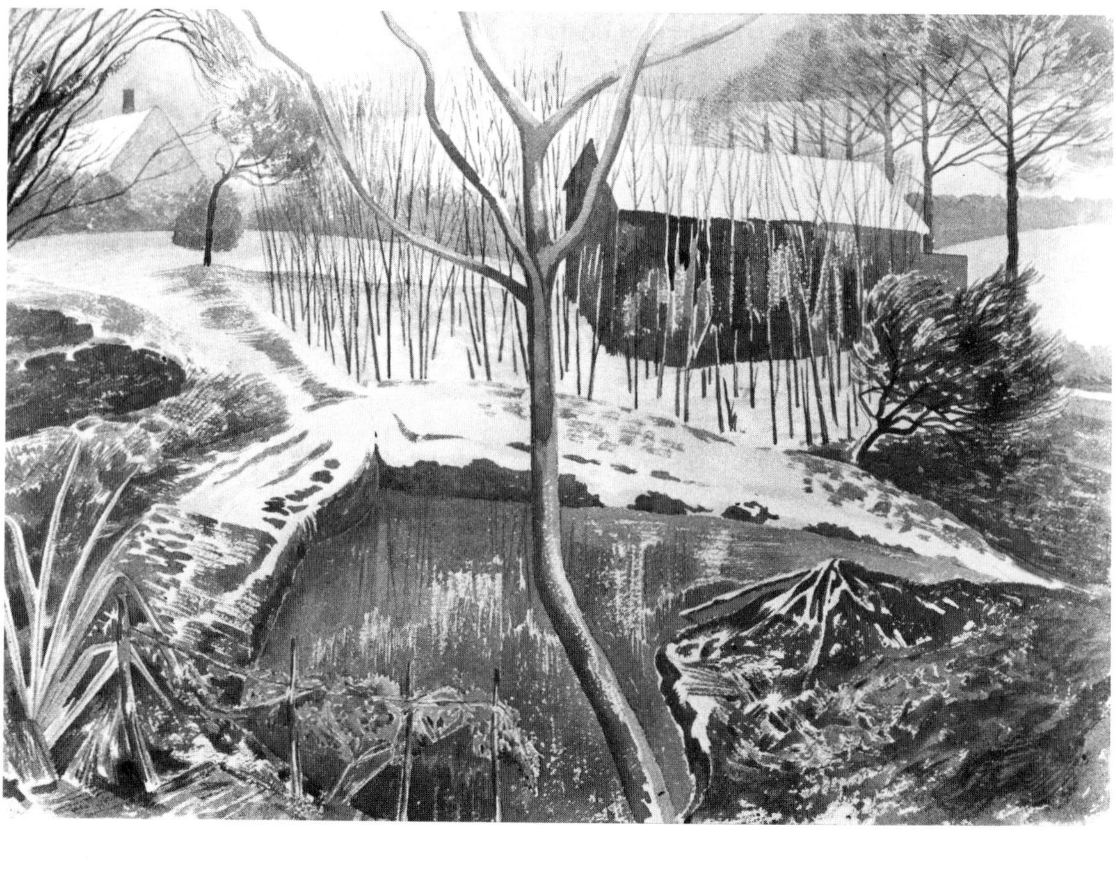

John Nash
Wild Garden, Winter
1959; watercolour
40·6 × 57·2 cm
Tate Gallery, London

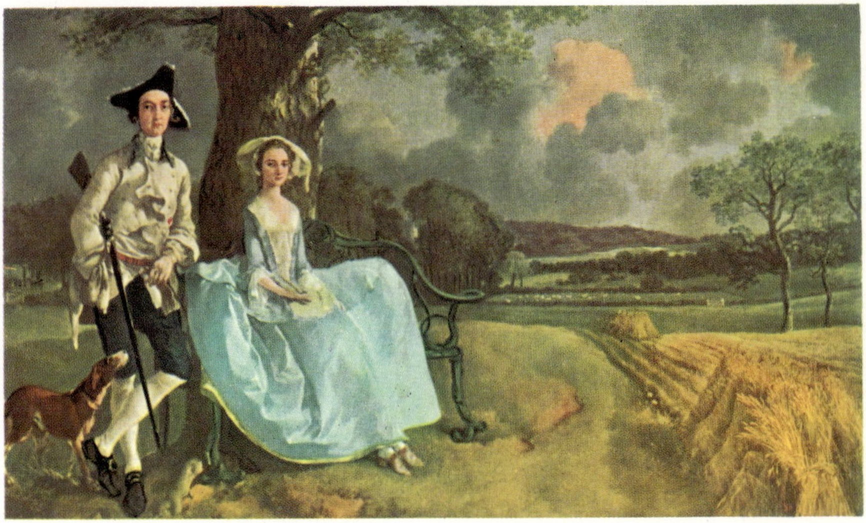

Thomas Gainsborough *Mr and Mrs Andrews* c. 1750; oil on canvas, 69·8 × 119·4 cm National Gallery, London

wife Christine did not move permanently to Suffolk until 1929, however, when they rented a bungalow next to Wormingford Mill. After this burnt down a year later, they lived in a thatched cottage (still surviving) at Winston, a hamlet on the road from Wormingford to Bures. They finally settled at Bottengols in 1943.

The life they led here was a remarkably simple one, and their domestic facilities were primitive; for a long period Bottengols was without electricity, and the only source of water was a stream which ran along an open culvert across the kitchen floor. Gradually improvements were made, including the diversion of the stream. Now the house survives almost in the condition in which Nash left it. It is surrounded by an exotic garden, which he assiduously cultivated over the years and which provided a major source of inspiration for his art: Nash was arguably the greatest botanical illustrator of recent times, and he taught the subject at the Flatford Mill Field Centre.

In spite of moving to the Stour Valley, Nash was never conscious of following in the footsteps of Constable. His reasons were much more prosaic: a postcard he wrote in July 1929 simply says: 'Good river scenery – think we might stay here.' His art expresses a spontaneous and humble response to nature, which contrasts completely with the self-consciously literary one of his brother.

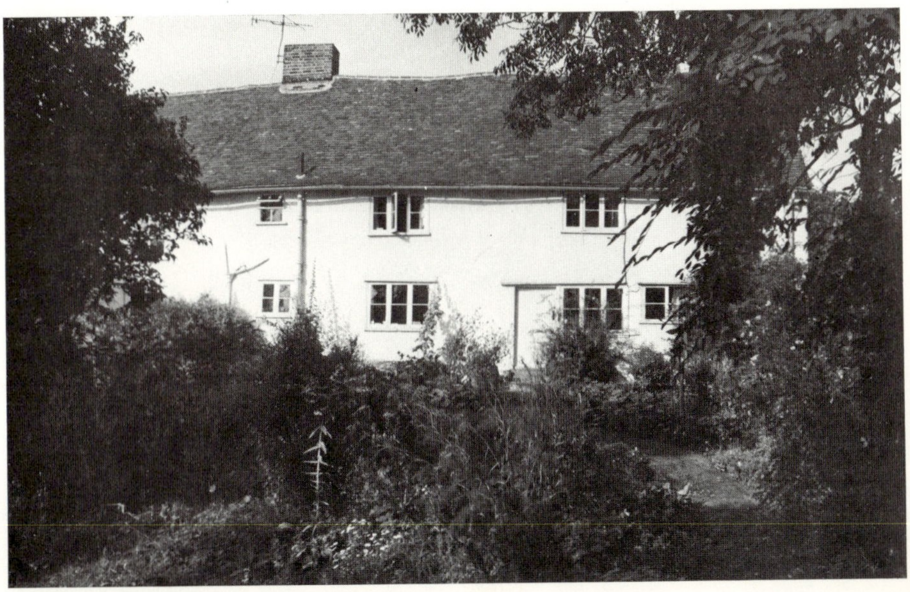

Bottengols, Wormingford (John Nash's house)